P O R

New
Orleans

by Mary Herczog

Macmillan • USA

ABOUT THE AUTHOR

Mary Herczog is a freelance writer who also works in the film industry. She is the author of *Frommer's Las Vegas,* and covered Bali for *Frommer's Southeast Asia.* She would never leave New Orleans if it weren't for July and August.

MACMILLAN TRAVEL

Macmillan General Reference USA, Inc.
1633 Broadway
New York, NY 10019

Find us online at **www.frommers.com**

ISBN 0-02-863056-4
ISSN 1090-316X

Editor: Justin Lapatine
Production Editor: Christina Van Camp
Photo Editor: Richard Fox
Design by Michele Laseau
Staff Cartographers: John Decamillis and Roberta Stockwell
Page creation by John Bitter, Ellen Considine, and Natalie Evans

SPECIAL SALES

Bulk purchases (10+ copies) of Frommer's and selected Macmillan travel guides are available to corporations, organizations, mail-order catalogs, institutions, and charities at special discounts, and can be customized to suit individual needs. For more information, write to Special Sales, Macmillan General Reference, 1633 Broadway, New York, NY 10019.

Manufactured in the United States of America

5   4   3   2   1

Contents

List of Maps

AN INVITATION TO THE READER

In researching this book, we discovered many wonderful places, hotels, restaurants, shops, and more. We're sure you'll find others. Please tell us about them, so we can share the information with your fellow travelers in upcoming editions. If you were disappointed with a recommendation, we'd love to know that, too. Please write to:

Frommer's Portable New Orleans 2000
Macmillan Travel
1633 Broadway
New York, NY 10019

AN ADDITIONAL NOTE

Please be advised that travel information is subject to change at any time—and this is especially true of prices. We therefore suggest that you write or call ahead for confirmation when making your travel plans. The authors, editors, and publisher cannot be held responsible for the experiences of readers while traveling. Your safety is important to us, however, so we encourage you to stay alert and be aware of your surroundings. Keep a close eye on cameras, purses, and wallets, all favorite targets of thieves and pickpockets.

WHAT THE SYMBOLS MEAN
✪ Frommer's Favorites

Our favorite places and experiences, outstanding for quality, value, or both.

The following abbreviations are used for credit cards:

AE	American Express	EURO	Eurocard
CB	Carte Blanche	JCB	Japan Credit Bank
DC	Diners Club	MC	MasterCard
DISC	Discover	V	Visa
ER	enRoute		

FIND FROMMER'S ONLINE

Arthur Frommer's Budget Travel Online (www.frommers.com) offers more than 6,000 pages of up-to-the-minute travel information—including the latest bargains and candid, personal articles updated daily by Arthur Frommer himself. No other Web site offers such comprehensive and timely coverage of the world of travel.

Planning a Trip to New Orleans

With the possible exception of July and August (unless you thrive on heat and humidity), just about any time is the right time to go to New Orleans. Whatever your idea of the ideal New Orleans trip, this chapter will give you the information to make informed plans, and will point you toward some additional resources.

1 Visitor Information & Money

VISITOR INFORMATION

Even a seasoned traveler should considering writing or calling ahead to the **New Orleans Metropolitan Convention and Visitors Bureau,** 1520 Sugar Bowl Dr., New Orleans, LA 70112 (☎ **800/672-6124** or 504/566-5055; www.nawlins.com; e-mail: tourism@nawlins.com). The staff is extremely friendly and helpful, and you can easily get any information you can't find in this book from them.

Another source of information is **the Greater New Orleans Black Tourism Network,** Louisiana Superdome, 1520 Sugar Bowl Dr. 70112 (☎ **504/523-5652**); you may be particularly interested in their self-directed tours of African American landmarks.

SITE SEEING: THE BIG EASY ON THE WEB

The following Web sites offer buckets of useful information—and, in some cases, personal opinions—on New Orleans activities, lodgings, restaurants, music, nightlife, food, culture, eccentricities, and just about anything else you can think of.

- **www.nolalive.com** The *Times-Picayune's* site for locals. The newspaper offers good food reviews and local fest information.
- **www.loveneworleans.com** The tourist version of the above, featuring the infamous "Bourbocam": a video camera trained 24 hours a day on Bourbon Street.
- **www.gumbopages.com** Expatriate Chuck Taggart has packed the Gumbo Pages with nearly everything about New Orleans music and food.

- **www.neosoft.com/~offbeat**   *Offbeat* magazine's site is probably the most comprehensive source of music listings. It's chock-full of info and in-the-know local artist information, plus a dense links page.
- **www.gayneworleans.com**   This site provides information on lodging, dining, arts, and nightlife, and links to other information on New Orleans gay life.
- **http://citylink.neosoft.com/citylink/mardigr**   The "official" Mardi Gras site.
- **www.nojazzfest.com**   The Jazz and Heritage Festival's official site. Goes dormant after May, and starts up again a couple months before the event.

MONEY

Prices for everything from accommodations to zydeco clubs go up precipitously during major events and festivals (see chapter 2). New Orleans is also quite popular in the fall, during what has become the convention season. The heat and humidity of the summer months (July and August) keep tourism in the city to its yearly low, so if the weather doesn't bother you, you can find some incredible bargains, especially at hotels.

You can get traveler's checks at almost any bank. **American Express** offers denominations of $10, $20, $50, $100, $500, and $1,000. You'll pay a service charge ranging from 1 to 4 percent. You can also get American Express traveler's checks over the phone by calling ☎ **800/221-7282;** by using this number, Amex gold and platinum cardholders are exempt from the 1% fee. AAA members can obtain checks without a fee at most AAA offices.

Visa offers traveler's checks at Citibank locations nationwide, as well as several other banks. The service charge ranges between 1.5% and 2%; checks come in denominations of $20, $50, $100, $500, and $1,000. **MasterCard** also offers traveler's checks. Call ☎ **800/223-9920** for a location near you.

Most hotels will happily cash traveler's checks for you, while many stores and restaurants are equally pleased to accept them (as are even the food booths at Jazz Fest!). You can buy traveler's checks at most major banks, or from **American Express** (☎ **800/221-7282**).

There are automated-teller machines (ATMs) throughout New Orleans, most of which are connected to national ATM networks.

You might want to check with your bank before you leave home to see if it can provide a list of ATM locations that will accept your card. If your bank is connected to the **Plus** network, call ☎ **800/843-7587** for its ATM locator; for **Cirrus**, call ☎ **800/424-7787.** Some centrally located ATMs in New Orleans are at the First National Bank of Commerce, 240 Royal St.; Hibernia National Bank, 701 Poydras St.; and Whitney National Bank, 228 St. Charles Ave.

2 When to Go

THE WEATHER

The average mean temperature in New Orleans is an inviting 70°F, but it can drop or rise considerably in a single day. (We've experienced 40°F and rain one day, and 80°F and humidity the next.) Conditions depend primarily on two things: whether it rains and whether there is direct sunlight or cloud cover. Rain can provide slight and temporary relief on a hot day; for the most part, it hits in sudden (and sometimes dramatically heavy) showers, which disappear as quickly as they arrived. Anytime the sun shines unimpeded, it gets much warmer. The region's high humidity can make even mild warms and colds feel intense. Still, the city's semitropical climate is part of its appeal—a slight bit of moistness makes the air come sensually alive. It will be pleasant at almost any time of year except July and August, which can be exceptionally hot and muggy. If you do come during those months, you'll quickly learn to follow the natives' example, staying out of the noonday sun and ducking from one air-conditioned building to another. Winter is very mild by American standards, but is punctuated by an occasional cold snap, when the mercury can drop below the freezing point.

PACKING TIPS   In the dead of summer, T-shirts and shorts are absolutely acceptable everywhere except the finest restaurants. In the spring and fall, something a little warmer is in order; in the winter, you should plan to carry a lightweight coat or jacket. Umbrellas and cheap rain jackets are available everywhere for those tourists who inevitably get caught in a sudden, unexpected downpour.

New Orleans Average Temperatures & Rainfall

	Jan	Feb	Mar	Apr	May	June	July	Aug	Sept	Oct	Nov	Dec
High (°F)	69	65	71	79	85	90	91	90	87	79	70	64
High (°C)	21	18	22	26	29	32	33	32	30	26	21	18
Days of Rainfall	10	9	9	7	8	10	15	13	10	5	7	10

NEW ORLEANS CALENDAR OF EVENTS

For more information on **Mardi Gras, Jazz Fest, Festivals Acadiens,** and other major area events, see chapter 2. For general information, contact the **New Orleans Metropolitan Convention and Visitors Bureau,** 1520 Sugar Bowl Dr., New Orleans, LA 70112 (☎ **800/672-6124** or 504/566-5055; www.nawlins.com; e-mail: tourism@nawlins.com).

January

- The **USF&G Sugar Bowl Classic.** First held in 1934, this is New Orleans' oldest yearly sporting occasion. The football game is the main event, but there are also tennis, swimming, basketball, sailing, running, and flag-football competitions. Fans tend to be really loud, really boisterous, and everywhere during the festivities. For information, contact USF&G Insurance Sugar Bowl, 1500 Sugar Bowl Dr., New Orleans, LA 70112 (☎ **504/525-8573**). January 1.

March

- ✪ **Lundi Gras.** An old tradition that has been revived in the last decade or so. Celebrations take place at Spanish Plaza. It's free, it's outdoors, and it features music (including a jazz competition) and the arrival of Rex at 6pm, marking the beginning of Mardi Gras. For more information, contact New Orleans Riverwalk, 1 Poydras St., New Orleans, LA 70130 (☎ **504/522-1555**). Monday before Mardi Gras (in 2000, March 6).

- ✪ **Mardi Gras.** The culmination of the 2-month-long carnival season, Mardi Gras is the big annual blowout, a city-wide party that takes place on Fat Tuesday (the last day before Lent in the Christian calendar). The entire city stops working (sometimes days in advance!) and starts partying in the early morning. Day before Ash Wednesday (in 2000, March 7).

- **Black Heritage Festival.** Honors the various African American cultural contributions to New Orleans. Specific events usually begin about 2 weeks after Carnival. Write or call the Black Heritage Foundation, 4535 S. Prieur St., New Orleans, LA 70125 (☎ **504/827-0112**) for more info.

- **St. Patrick's Day Parades.** There are two. One takes place in the French Quarter, beginning at Molly's at the Market (1107 Decatur St.), and the other goes through the Irish Channel neighborhood, following a route that begins at Race and Annunciation streets and ends at Jackson Street. The parades have the flavor of Mardi Gras, but tinted green, with a corned-beef-and-cabbage undertone. For information on the French Quarter parade, call **Molly's at the Market** (☎ **504/525-5169**). The Irish Channel parade will be on March 13 in 2000.

✪ **Tennessee Williams New Orleans Literary Festival.** A 5-day series celebrating New Orleans' rich literary heritage, it includes theatrical performances, readings, discussion panels, master classes, musical events, and literary walking tours dedicated to the playwright. For information, call or write 5500 Prytania St., Suite 217, New Orleans, LA 70115 (☎ **504/581-1144**). Late March.

✪ **Spring Fiesta.** The fiesta, which begins with the crowning of the Spring Fiesta queen, is more than half a century old and takes place throughout the city. Historical and architectural tours of many of the city's private homes, courtyards, and plantation homes are offered in conjunction with the 5-day event. For the schedule, call or write the Spring Fiesta Association, 826 St. Ann St., New Orleans, LA 70116 (☎ **504/581-1367**). Late March and early April.

April

✪ The **French Quarter Festival.** This is a relatively new event, just over a decade old, that celebrates New Orleans' history. For hardcore jazz fans, it is rapidly becoming an alternative to Jazz Fest. It kicks off with a parade down Bourbon Street. Among other things, you can join people dancing in the streets, learn the history of jazz, visit historic homes, and take a ride on a riverboat. Many local restaurants set up booths in Jackson Square, so the eating is exceptionally good. Events are held all over the French Quarter. For information, call or write French Quarter Festivals, 100 Conti St., New Orleans, LA 70130 (☎ **504/522-5730**). Middle of the month.

✪ **The New Orleans Jazz & Heritage Festival.** A 10-day event that draws musicians, music fans, cooks, and craftspeople to celebrate music and life, Jazz Fest rivals Mardi Gras in popularity. Lodgings in the city tend to sell out up to a year ahead, so book early. Events take place at the Fair Grounds Race Track and various venues throughout the city. For information, call or write the **New Orleans Jazz and Heritage Festival,** 1205 N. Rampart St., New Orleans, LA 70116 (☎ **504/522-4786;** www.nojazzfest. com). Usually held the last weekend in April and first weekend in May.

- **The Crescent City Classic.** This 10K road race, from Jackson Square to Audubon Park, brings an international field of top runners to the city. For more information, call or write the Classic, 104 Metairie Heights Ave., Metairie, LA 70001 (☎ **504/861-8686**). Saturday before Easter (in 2000, April 22).

May

- **Greek Festival.** At the Holy Trinity Cathedral's Hellenic Cultural Center, it features Greek folk dancing, specialty foods, crafts, and music. For more information about the 3-day event, call or write Holy Trinity Cathedral, 1200 Robert E. Lee Blvd., New Orleans, LA 70122 (☎ **504/282-0259**). End of the month.

June

- **The Great French Market Tomato Festival.** A celebration of tomato diversity, this day-long event features cooking and tastings in the historic French Market. For more information, call or write the French Market, P.O. Box 51749, New Orleans, LA 70151 (☎ **504/522-2621**). First Sunday in June.
- **Reggae Riddums Festival.** This 3-day gathering of calypso, reggae, and soca (a blend of soul and calypso) musicians is held in City Park, and includes a heady helping of ethnic foods and arts and crafts. For more information, call or write Ernest Kelly, P.O. Box 6156, New Orleans, LA 70174 (☎ **888/767-1317** or 504/367-1313). Second week of the month.

July

- **Go Fourth on the River.** The annual Fourth of July celebration begins in the morning at the riverfront and continues into the night, culminating in a spectacular fireworks display. For more information, call or write Anna Pepper, 610 S. Peters St., Suite 301, New Orleans, LA 70130 (☎ **504/528-9994**).
- **New Orleans Wine and Food Experience.** Antique shops and art galleries throughout the French Quarter hold wine and food tastings, wine makers and local chefs conduct seminars, and a variety of vintner dinners and grand tastings are held for your gourmandistic pleasure. More than 150 wines and 40 restaurants are featured every day. For information, call or write Mary Reynolds, P.O. Box 70514, New Orleans, LA 70172 (☎ **504/529-9463**). End of the month.

September

- **Southern Decadence.** All over the French Quarter, thousands of folks—drag queens, mostly—follow a secret parade route, making sure to stop into many bars along the way. People travel from far and wide to be a part of the festivities. For information, try the Web site (www.southerndecadence.com) or contact **AmBush Magazine 2000,** 828-A Bourbon St., New Orleans, LA 70116-3137 (☎ **800/876-1484** or 504/522-8047; fax 504/522-0907). Sunday of Labor Day weekend.

- **Swamp Festival.** Sponsored by the Audubon Institute, the Swamp Festival features long days of live swamp music performances (lots of good zydeco here) as well as hands-on contact with Louisiana swamp animals. Admission to the festival is free with zoo admission. For information, call or write the Audubon Institute, 6500 Magazine St., New Orleans, LA 70118 (☎ **504/861-2537**). Last weekend in September and first weekend in October.

October

- **Art for Arts' Sake.** The arts season begins with gallery openings throughout the city. Julia, Magazine, and Royal streets are where the action is. For more information, contact the Contemporary Arts Center, 900 Camp St., New Orleans, LA 70130 (☎ **504/523-1216**). Lasts throughout month.

- **Louisiana Jazz Awareness Month.** There are nightly concerts (some of which are free), television and radio specials, and lectures, all sponsored by the Louisiana Jazz Federation. For more information and a schedule, contact the Louisiana Jazz Federation, 225 Baronne St., Suite 1712, New Orleans, LA 70112 (☎ **504/522-3154**).

- **New Orleans Film and Video Festival.** This relatively young festival is well worth checking out. Canal Place Cinemas and other theaters throughout the city screen award-winning local and international films and host writers, actors, and directors over the course of a week. Admission prices range from $3 to $12. For dates, contact the New Orleans Film and Video Society, 225 Baronne St., Suite 1712, New Orleans, LA 70112 (☎ **504/523-3818;** www.neworleansfilmfest.com; e-mail: neworleansfilmfest@wordnet.att.net). Midmonth.

✪ **Halloween.** Rivaling Mardi Gras in terms of costumes, Halloween is certainly celebrated more grandly here than in any other American city. After all, New Orleans has a way with ghosts. Events include Boo-at-the-Zoo (October 30 and 31) for children, costume parties (including a Monster Bash at the Ernest N. Morial Convention Center), haunted houses (one of the best is run by the sheriff's department in City Park), the Anne Rice Vampire Lestat Extravaganza, and the Moonlight Witches Run. You can catch the ghoulish action all over the city—many museums get in on the fun with specially designed tours—but the French Quarter, as always, is the center of the Halloween-night universe. October 31.

December

- **A New Orleans Christmas.** Holiday events include candlelight caroling in Jackson Square; old New Orleans homes are dressed up especially for the occasion. Restaurants offer specially created multicourse Reveilion dinners, and hotels throughout the city offer "Papa Noël" rates. For information, contact French Quarter Festivals, 100 Conti St., New Orleans, LA 70130 (☎ **504/522-5730**). All month.

- **Celebration in the Oaks.** Lights and lighted figures, designed to illustrate holiday themes, bedeck sections of City Park. Driving tours are $5 per family car or van, and walking tours are $3 per person. For information, contact Celebration in the Oaks, 1 Palm Dr., New Orleans, LA 70124 (☎ **504/483-9415**). Late November to early January.

- **New Year's Eve.** The countdown takes place in Jackson Square and is one of the country's biggest and most reliable street parties. In the South-coast equivalent of New York's Times Square, revelers watch a lighted ball drop from the top of Jackson Brewery. December 31.

3 Getting There

BY PLANE

No fewer than 13 airlines fly to New Orleans' **Moisant International Airport** (airline code **MSY,** for those of you browsing fares on the Web), among them **American** (☎ 800/433-7300; www.aa.com), **Continental** (☎ 800/525-0280 or 504/581-2965; www.flycontiental.com), **Delta** (☎ 800/221-1212; www.delta-air.com), **Northwest** (☎ 800/225-2525; www.nwa.com), **Southwest**

(☎ 800/435-9792; www.iflyswa.com), **TWA** (☎ 504/529-2585; www2.twa.com), and **US Airways** (☎ 800/428-4322; www. usairways.com). The airport is 15 miles west of the city, in Kenner. You'll find information booths scattered around the airport and in the baggage claim area. There's also a branch of the **Travelers Aid Society** (☎ 504/464-3522).

BY CAR

You can drive to New Orleans via **I-10, I-55, U.S. 90,** and **U.S. 61** and across the Lake Pontchartrain Causeway on **La. 25.** From any direction, you'll see the city's distinctive and swampy outlying regions; if you can, try to drive in while you can enjoy the scenery in daylight. For the best roadside views, take U.S. 61 or La. 25, but only if you have time to spare. The larger roads are considerably faster.

It's a good idea to call before you leave home to ask for directions to your hotel. Most hotels have parking facilities (for a fee); if they don't, they'll give you the names and addresses of nearby parking lots.

AAA (☎ 800/926-4222) will assist members with trip planning and emergency services.

CAR RENTALS   Driving in New Orleans can be a hassle, and parking is a nightmare. Cabs are plentiful, and not too expensive, so you don't need a car in New Orleans unless you're planning several day trips. Nevertheless, most major national car rental companies are represented at the airport, including **Alamo** (☎ 800/327-9633), **Avis** (☎ 800/331-1212), **Budget** (☎ 800/527-0700), **Dollar** (☎ 800/800-4000), **Hertz** (☎ 800/654-3131), and **National** (☎ 800/227-7368).

BY TRAIN

Amtrak (☎ 800/USA-RAIL or 504/528-1610) trains serve New Orleans' **Union Passenger Terminal,** 1001 Loyola Ave., from Los Angeles and intermediate points; from New York, Washington, and points in between; and from Chicago and intermediate points. Using All Aboard America fares, you'll pay $188 to $208 from New York or Chicago, $248 to $288 from Los Angeles. Amtrak frequently offers senior-citizen discounts and other packages, some with a rental car, so be sure to check when you reserve. Also, many Amtrak discounts depend on early reservations.

Amtrak also offers some appealing tour packages, which can be arranged through your local Amtrak Tour Desk. Options include a ticket with accommodations, an air-rail package—take the train and then fly back home—and eight other combinations of tour packages.

The New Orleans train station is in the Central Business District. Plenty of taxis wait outside the main entrance to the passenger terminal. Hotels in the French Quarter and the Central Business District are a short ride away.

BY BUS

Greyhound-Trailways buses (☎ **800/231-2222** or 504/524-7571) come into the **Union Passenger Terminal** from points throughout the country. The terminal is located at 1001 Loyola Ave., in the Central Business District. We recommend taking a cab from the bus terminal to your hotel. There should be taxis out front, but if there aren't, the number for **United Cabs** is ☎ **504/522-9771.**

4 For Foreign Visitors

ENTRY REQUIREMENTS

Immigration laws are a hot political issue in the United States these days, and the following requirements may have changed somewhat by the time you plan your trip. Check at any U.S. embassy or consulate for current information and requirements. You can also plug into the **U.S. State Department's** Internet site at **http://state.gov**.

The U.S. State Department has a **Visa Waiver Pilot Program** allowing citizens of certain countries to enter the United States without a visa for stays of up to 90 days. At press time these included Andorra, Argentina, Australia, Austria, Belgium, Brunei, Denmark, Finland, France, Germany, Iceland, Ireland, Italy, Japan, Liechtenstein, Luxembourg, Monaco, the Netherlands, New Zealand, Norway, San Marino, Slovenia, Spain, Sweden, Switzerland, and the United Kingdom. Citizens of these countries need only a valid passport and a round-trip air or cruise ticket in their possession upon arrival. If they first enter the United States, they may also visit Mexico, Canada, Bermuda, and/or the Caribbean islands and return to the United States without a visa. Further information is available from any U.S. embassy or consulate. Canadian citizens may enter the United States without visas; they need only proof of residence.

Citizens of all other countries must have (1) a valid passport that expires at least 6 months later than the scheduled end of their visit to the United States, and (2) a tourist visa, which may be obtained without charge from any U.S. consulate.

Usually you can obtain a visa at once or within 24 hours, but it may take longer during the summer rush from June through August. If you cannot go in person, contact the nearest U.S. embassy or consulate for directions on applying by mail. Your travel agent or airline office may also be able to provide you with visa applications and instructions. The U.S. consulate or embassy that issues your visa will determine whether you will be issued a multiple- or single-entry visa and any restrictions regarding the length of your stay.

British subjects can obtain up-to-date passport and visa information by calling the **U.S. Embassy Visa Information Line** (☎ **0891/ 200-290**) or the **London Passport Office** (☎ **0990/210-410** for recorded information).

Telephone operators will answer your inquiries regarding U.S. immigration policies or laws at the **Immigration and Naturalization Service's Customer Information Center** (☎ **800/375-5283**). Representatives are available from 9am to 3pm, Monday through Friday. The INS also runs a 24-hour automated information service, for commonly asked questions, at ☎ **800/755-0777.**

MEDICAL REQUIREMENTS

Unless you're arriving from an area known to be suffering from an epidemic (particularly cholera or yellow fever), inoculations or vaccinations are not required for entry into the United States. If you have a disease that requires treatment with narcotics or syringe-administered medications, carry a valid signed prescription from your physician to allay any suspicions that you may be smuggling narcotics (a serious offense that carries severe penalties in the U.S.).

For HIV-positive visitors, requirements for entering the United States are somewhat vague and change frequently. For up-to-the-minute information concerning HIV-positive travelers, contact the Centers for Disease Control's **National Center for HIV** (☎ **404/ 332-4559;** www.hivatis.org) or the **Gay Men's Health Crisis** (☎ **212/367-1000;** www.gmhc.org).

CUSTOMS REQUIREMENTS

Every visitor over 21 years of age may bring in, free of duty, the following: (1) 1 liter of wine or hard liquor; (2) 200 cigarettes or 100 cigars (but not from Cuba) or 3 pounds of smoking tobacco; and (3) $100 worth of gifts. These exemptions are offered to travelers who spend at least 72 hours in the United States and who have not claimed them within the preceding 6 months. It is altogether forbidden to bring into the country foodstuffs (particularly fruit, cooked meats, and canned goods) and plants (vegetables, seeds, tropical plants, and the like). Foreign tourists may bring in or take out up to $10,000 in U.S. or foreign currency with no formalities; larger sums must be declared to U.S. Customs on entering or leaving. For more specific information regarding U.S. Customs, call your nearest U.S. embassy or consulate, or the **U.S. Customs** office at ☎ **202/927-1770** or www.customs.ustreas.gov.

Foreign tourists to Louisiana can receive a refund on taxes paid on tangible goods purchased within the state. You must show your passport (Canadians can show a driver's license) at the time of purchase and *request a tax refund voucher from the vendor.* You will be charged the full amount and given a sales receipt and a refund voucher. If you're leaving New Orleans by plane, go to the Louisiana Tax Free Shopping Refund Center at the airport. Present your sales receipts and vouchers from merchants, your passport, and a round-trip international ticket (the duration of the trip must be less than 90 days). To arrange your refund by mail, you'll need copies of sales receipts, copies of your travel ticket and passport, your original refund vouchers, and a statement explaining why you were not able to claim your refund at the airport. Send these to: **Louisiana Tax Free Shopping Refund Center,** P.O. Box 20125, New Orleans, LA 70141 (☎ **504/467-0723**).

INSURANCE

Although it's not required of travelers, health insurance is highly recommended. Unlike many European countries, the United States does not usually offer free or low-cost medical care to its citizens or visitors. Doctors and hospitals are expensive, and in most cases will require advance payment or proof of coverage before they render their services. Policies can cover everything from the loss or theft of your baggage and trip cancellation to the guarantee of bail in case you're arrested. Good policies will also cover the costs of an accident, repatriation, or death. Packages such as **Europ Assistance** in Europe are sold by automobile clubs and travel agencies at attractive rates. **Worldwide Assistance Services,** Inc. (☎ **800/821-2828**) is the agent for Europ Assistance in the United States. Though lack of health insurance may prevent you from being admitted to a hospital in nonemergencies, don't worry about being left on a street corner to die: the American way is to fix you now and bill the living daylights out of you later.

MONEY

CURRENCY & EXCHANGE   The U.S. monetary system is painfully simple: The most common bills (all ugly, all green) are the $1 (colloquially, a "buck"), $5, $10, and $20 denominations. There are also $2 bills (seldom encountered), $50 bills, and $100 bills (the last two are usually not welcome as payment for small purchases). The $100, $50, and $20 bills have been redesigned in the past few years, with changes to the $10 and $5 expected in 2000. Despite rumors to the contrary, both the old and the new versions of all bills are still legal tender.

There are six denominations of coins: 1¢ (1 cent, or a penny); 5¢ (5 cents, or a nickel); 10¢ (10 cents, or a dime); 25¢ (25 cents, or a quarter); 50¢ (50 cents, or a half dollar); and, prized by collectors, the rare $1 piece (the older, large silver dollar and the newer, small Susan B. Anthony coin). A new gold $1 piece will be introduced by the year 2000.

Note: The "foreign-exchange bureaus" so common in Europe are rare even at airports in the United States, and nonexistent outside major cities. It's best not to change foreign money (or traveler's checks denominated in a currency other than U.S. dollars) at a small-town bank, or even a branch in a big city; in fact, leave any currency other than U.S. dollars at home—it may prove a greater nuisance to you than it's worth.

SAFETY

While tourist areas are generally safe, crime is on the increase everywhere, and U.S. urban areas tend to be less safe than those in Europe or Japan. Visitors should always stay alert. This is particularly true of large U.S. cities. In New Orleans, avoid deserted areas (like the outer edges of the French Quarter), especially at night. Don't go into any cemeteries or city parks at night unless there's an event that attracts crowds, like a festival or concert. Generally speaking, you can feel safe in areas where there are many people and many open establishments. Contact the New Orleans Metropolitan Convention and Visitors Bureau if you're in doubt about which neighborhoods are safe.

Avoid carrying valuables with you on the street, and don't display expensive cameras or electronic equipment. Hold on to your pocketbook and place your billfold in an inside pocket. In theaters, restaurants, and other public places, keep your possessions in sight.

2

Mardi Gras & Other Festivals

*T*his is a city that really loves a good party. And what happens when a party gets too big? It becomes a festival. That's what has happened over the years to the Jazz and Heritage Festival. Anything is an excuse for a party, and so you can experience festivals centered around swamps, gumbo, crawfish, frogs, tomatoes, and architecture. New Orleanians know what makes a great party: really good food and music, and lots of it. That's what you will find at any festival in Louisiana, regardless of what it is ostensibly celebrating.

This chapter covers some of the largest festivals in New Orleans and the outlying areas; others are listed in the "New Orleans Calendar of Events" in chapter 1. You can get information on many of the events mentioned in both chapters by contacting the **New Orleans Metropolitan Convention and Visitors Bureau,** 1520 Sugar Bowl Dr., New Orleans, LA 70112 (☎ **800/672-6124** or 504/566-5055; www.nawlins.com; e-mail: tourism@nawlins.com). Be sure to ask the people at the bureau if any other events are scheduled during your visit.

1 Mardi Gras

Obviously, the granddaddy of all New Orleans celebrations is Mardi Gras. Thanks to sensational media accounts that zero in on the salacious portions, Mardi Gras' rep has gone downhill in the last few years—while the accounts have attracted more and more participants looking for wild action rather than tradition. But despite what you may have heard, Mardi Gras remains one of the most exciting times to visit this city. You can spend several days admiring and reveling in the traditions and never even venture into the frat-party atmosphere of Bourbon Street.

First of all, it's not a festival; it's a "carnival," from a Latin word roughly meaning "farewell to flesh." Mardi Gras is French for "Fat Tuesday," the day before Ash Wednesday, when Lent begins, and historically refers to the 5- to 8-week stretch from Twelfth Night (January 6) to Mardi Gras day (which can fall as late as March 9). With Lent comes fasting and deprivation. The idea was that good

Christians would take the opportunity to eat as much as they could in preparation for their impending denial.

KICKIN' UP YOUR HEELS: MARDI GRAS ACTIVITIES

One of the beautiful things about Mardi Gras, residents point out, is that with a mask on your face, you can be and do anything you want. You feel the total freedom of anonymity.

In that same way, Mardi Gras itself can be whatever you want. Don't be suckered by media reports that focus on the exhibitionism and drunken orgies. Sure, some of Mardi Gras is becoming more and more like spring break, as college kids pour into town, eager to have license to do anything. Thankfully, that kind of activity is largely confined to Bourbon Street. If that's what you want, go there. But if you avoid Bourbon Street, you will find an entirely different Mardi Gras experience.

THE SEASON   The date of Fat Tuesday is different each year, but carnival season always starts on Twelfth Night, January 6, as much as 2 months before Mardi Gras. On that night, the Phunny Phorty Phellows kick off the season with a streetcar ride from Carrollton to Canal Street and back.

Over the following weeks, the city celebrates Mardi Gras in its own inimitable fashion. For most people, this means attending a string of King Cake parties. The traditional King Cake is a round, braided confection into which a plastic baby is baked; getting the piece with the baby can be a good omen or can mean you have to throw the next King Cake party. For the high society crowd, the season brings the year's best parties, some of which hark back to the grand masked balls of the 19th century. Each krewe throws a ball, ostensibly to introduce its royalty for the year. There are dozens of these parties between Twelfth Night and Mardi Gras, but most are not traditional masked balls. (By the way, don't expect to be invited—they are quite exclusive.)

As the season progresses, the hazy outline of Mardi Gras becomes apparent, and things start to get more and more festive. Two or three weeks before Mardi Gras itself, parades begin chugging through the streets with increasing frequency. If you want to experience Mardi Gras but don't want to face the full force of craziness, consider coming for the weekend 10 days before Fat Tuesday (the season officially begins the Friday of this weekend). You can count on 10 to 15 parades during the weekend, by lesser-known krewes like Cleopatra, Pontchartrain, Sparta, and Camelot. The crowds are more manageable than the ones you'll find just a week later.

That following weekend there are another 15 parades—the biggies. Everything's bigger: the parades are bigger, the crowds are bigger, everything's bigger. By this point, the city has succumbed to carnival fever. After a day of screaming for beads, you'll probably find yourself heading somewhere to get a drink or three. The French Quarter will be the center of late-night revelry; all of the larger bars will be packed. If you go uptown or to Mid City to see a parade, however, you might consider staying put and spending your evening at one of the joints nearby. The last parade each day (on both weekends) usually ends around 9:30pm or later; if you have children along, they'll probably be beat by the time you get back to the hotel. You might be, too.

By the way, a good Mardi Gras activity for children is a trip to the Mardi Gras Museum in Kenner's Rivertown area (see chapter 6).

LUNDI GRAS   In the 19th century, Rex's King of Carnival arrived downtown from the Mississippi River on this night, the Monday before Fat Tuesday. Over the years, the day gradually lost its special significance, becoming just another day of parades. In the 1980s, however, Rex revived the old tradition.

These days, festivities at the riverfront begin in the afternoon, with lots of drink and live music leading up to the King's arrival at around 6pm. Down the levee a few hundred feet, at Wolfenberg Park, Zulu has its own Lundi Gras celebration, with the king arriving at around 5pm. In 1999, for the first time, King Zulu met up with Rex, in an impressive ceremony. That night, the **Krewe of Orpheus** holds their parade. It's one of the biggest and most popular parades, thanks to the generosity of their throws. And although it's a recent addition to the Mardi Gras scene (it began in 1994), it holds fast to old Mardi Gras traditions, including floats designed by master float creator Henri Schindler.

Because Lent begins the following night at midnight, Monday is the final dusk-to-dawn night of Mardi Gras. A good portion of the city forgoes sleep so as not to waste the occasion—which only adds to the craziness.

MARDI GRAS   The day begins early, starting with the two biggest parades, **Zulu** and **Rex,** which run back to back. Zulu starts near the Central Business District at 8:30am, Rex starts Uptown at 10am.

Throughout the early morning, in between the parades, you can also see the elaborately costumed Mardi Gras **"walking clubs,"** like the Jefferson City Buzzards, the Pete Fountain Half Fast, and the Mondo Kayo Social and Marching Club (identifiable by their tropical/banana theme). They walk, they drink, they're usually accompanied by marching bands, and they probably didn't sleep the night before, so they don't move very fast. You can catch these "marchers" anywhere along their St. Charles Avenue route (between Poydras and Washington).

It will be early afternoon when Rex spills into the Central Business District. Nearby, at about this time, you can find some of the most elusive New Orleans figures, the **Mardi Gras Indians.** The "tribes" of New Orleans are small communities of African Americans and black Creoles (some of whom have Native American ancestors), mostly from the inner city. Their elaborate (and that's an understatement) beaded and feathered costumes, rivaling Bob Mackie Vegas headdresses in outrageousness and size, are entirely made by hand. Throughout the day, tribes of Indians from all over town converge along the median of Claiborne Avenue, underneath the interstate, where a large crowd of locals is always milling around to see the spectacle. If two tribes meet on the median, or back in their neighborhoods, they'll stage a mock confrontation, resettling their territory and common borders. (If you're lucky, you can sometimes catch these confrontations during other times of the year, if the Indians are out to celebrate something else, like Jazz Fest or the mayor's inauguration.)

In the Quarter, the frat-party action is largely confined to Bourbon Street. The more interesting activity is in the lower Quarter and the Frenchmen section of the Faubourg Marigny, where the artists and gay community really know how to celebrate Mardi Gras. The costumes are elaborate works of art, some the product of months of work. Although the people may be (okay, probably *will* be) drunk, they are boisterous and enthusiastic, not (for the most part) obnoxious.

As you make your way through the streets, keep your eyes peeled for members of the legendary Krewe of Comus. They will be men dressed in tuxes, with brooms over their shoulders, holding cowbells. Ask them if they are Comus, and they will deny it, insisting they are Cowbellians. But then they might hand you a vintage Comus doubloon, and the truth will be out.

If you can, try to stay until midnight, when the police come through the Quarter, officially shutting down Mardi Gras.

PLANNING A VISIT DURING MARDI GRAS

LODGING   You can't just drop in on Mardi Gras. If you do, you may find yourself sleeping in Jackson Square or on a sidewalk somewhere. Accommodations in the city and the nearby suburbs are booked solid, *so make your plans well ahead and book a room as early as possible.* Many people plan a year or more in advance. Prices are usually much higher during Mardi Gras, and most hotels and guest houses impose minimum-stay requirements.

CLOTHING   As with anything in New Orleans, but perhaps now more than ever, you must join in if you want to have the best time. Simply being a spectator is not enough. And that means a costume and mask. (Tellingly, the Bourbon Street participants usually do not wear costumes.)

If you've come unprepared, several shops in town specialize in Mardi Gras costumes and masks. One of the most reasonable is the **Mardi Gras Center,** 831 Chartres St. (☎ **504/524-4384**). If you come early enough, they can custom-make a costume to your specifications; if not, they're well stocked with new and used costumes, wigs, masks, hats, and makeup. You might also try the second-hand stores along Magazine Street, which have a large inventory of costumes from the year before. You can usually pick up something quite snazzy for not very much money.

DINING   If you want to eat at a restaurant during Mardi Gras, make reservations as early as possible. And pay very close attention to parade routes, because if there is one between you and your restaurant, you may not be able to cross the parade route and you can kiss your dinner goodbye. For those of you who don't plan in advance, this might work to your advantage; often restaurants have a high no-show rate during Mardi Gras for this reason, and a well-timed drop-in may work nicely.

PARKING   Remember that while the huge crowds you'll find everywhere add to the general merriment, they also grind traffic to a halt all over town. So our admonition against renting a car is even stronger during Mardi Gras. *Don't drive.* Instead, relax and take a cab or walk. Go with the flow. Don't get irritated. Parking along a parade route is not allowed 2 hours before and 2 hours after the parade. In addition, although you'll see people leaving their cars on "neutral ground" (the median strip), it's illegal to park there, and chances are good that you'll be towed. Traffic in New Orleans is never worse than in the hour after a parade.

Catch Them If You Can: Tips on Getting the Best Throws

Trust us, you're going to go crazy for beads, plastic cups, aluminum coins, and other "throws."

Now, if there's a trick to bead catching, we are darned if we know it. One surefire way is to be a small child or a cute college girl (or even better, a cute college girl sitting on a tall person's shoulders). If you are none of these, you must plead and beg and whine like everybody else. Direct eye contact with a float rider also works. Sob stories invoking real and fictional ailments and family members can't hurt—if you can make yourself heard above the din of everyone else's tale of woe and deservedness.

We don't condone the popular pastime of flashing body parts in exchange for beads. Neither does the city of New Orleans, which, in an effort to reclaim Mardi Gras from the party hearty types, has sternly asked float riders not to throw to exhibitionists.

Note: When beads land on the ground, put your foot over them to claim them, because if you reach for them with your hands you might well get your fingers broken by someone else stepping on them. If you get lucky and are tossed a whole package of beads, don't be greedy—share with your neighbors, who might well trade you a nifty strand in exchange.

SAFEKEEPING   Many, many cops are out, making the walk from uptown to downtown safer than at other times of year, but, not surprisingly, the streets of New Orleans are a haven for pickpockets during Mardi Gras. Take precautions.

PARADE WATCHING   There are two environments for viewing each parade. You can choose to stay downtown in the thick of the action, or you can walk out into the neighborhood the parade will traverse. There are still crowds Uptown and in Mid City, but they're not as large or rowdy as those farther downtown—and they're much more family oriented. Generally, the best place to watch parades is on St. Charles Avenue, between Napoleon and Jackson avenues, where the crowds are somewhat smaller and consist mostly of local families and college students.

CAJUN MARDI GRAS

Mardi Gras in New Orleans sounds like too much for you, no matter how low-key you keep it? Consider driving out to Cajun country, where Mardi Gras traditions are just as strong but considerably more, er, wholesome. Lafayette, the capital of French Acadiana, celebrates carnival in a different manner, one that reflects the Cajun heritage and spirit. Three full days of activities lead up to Cajun Mardi Gras, making it second in size only to New Orleans' celebration. There's one *big* difference, though: The Cajuns open their final pageant and ball to the general public. Don your formal wear and join right in!

Instead of Rex and his queen, the Lafayette festivities are ruled by King Gabriel and Queen Evangeline. They are the fictional hero and heroine of Henry Wadsworth Longfellow's epic poem "Evangeline," which was based on real-life lovers who were separated during the British expulsion of Acadians from Nova Scotia, around the time of the French and Indian War. Their story is still very much alive here, among the descendants of those who shared their wanderings.

Things get off to a joyous start with the Children's Krewe and Krewe of Bonaparte parades and ball, held on the Saturday before Mardi Gras, following a full day of celebration at Acadian Village. On Monday night, Queen Evangeline is honored at the Queen's Parade. The King's Parade, held the following morning, honors King Gabriel and opens a full day of merriment. Lafayette's African American community stages the Parade of King Toussaint L'Ouverture and Queen Suzanne Simonne at about noon, just after the King's Parade. Then the Krewe of Lafayette invites everyone to get into the act as its parade winds through the streets. Krewe participants trot along on foot or ride in the vehicle of their choice—some very imaginative modes of transportation turn up every year. The Mardi Gras climax, a formal ball presided over by the king and queen and their royal court, takes place that night. Everything stops promptly at midnight, as Cajuns and visitors alike depart to begin their observance of Lent.

In the Cajun countryside that surrounds Lafayette, there's yet another form of Mardi Gras celebration, one tied to the rural lifestyle. Cajuns firmly believe in sharing, so you're welcome to come along. The celebration goes like this: Bands of masked men dressed in raggedy patchwork costumes and peaked hats known as *capichons* set off on Mardi Gras morning on horseback, led by their *capitaine.* They ride from farm to farm, asking at each, *"Voulez-vous reçevoir le Mardi Gras?"* ("Will you receive the Mardi Gras?") and dismounting as the invariable "Oui" comes in reply. Each farmyard then becomes a miniature festival as the revelers *faire le macaque* ("make monkeyshines"), with song and dance, much drinking of beer, and other antics loosely labeled "entertainment." As payment for their show, they demand, and get, "a fat little chicken to make a big gumbo" (or sometimes a bag of rice or other ingredients).

When each band has visited its allotted farmyards, they all head back to town, where everyone else has already begun the general festivities. There'll be dancing in the streets, rowdy card games, storytelling, and the like until the wee hours, and you can be sure that all those fat little chickens go into the "gumbo gros" pot to make a very big gumbo indeed.

You can write or call ahead for particulars on both the urban and the rural Mardi Gras celebrations. For the latter, the towns of Eunice and Mamou stage some of the most enjoyable celebrations. Contact the **Lafayette Parish Convention and Visitors Commission Center,** P.O. Box 52066, Lafayette, LA 70505 (☎ **800/346-1958** in the U.S., 800/543-5340 in Canada, or 318/232-3808).

2 The New Orleans Jazz & Heritage Festival

What began in 1969 as a small gathering in a public park to celebrate the music of New Orleans now ranks as one of the best-attended, most-respected, and musically comprehensive festivals in the world. Although people call it "Jazz Fest," the full name is the New Orleans Jazz and Heritage Festival, and the heritage is about as broad as it can get. Stand in the right place and, depending on which way the wind's blowing, you can catch as many as 10 musical styles from several continents, smell the tantalizing aromas of a dozen or so different food offerings, and meet a U.N.–like spectrum of fellow fest-goers all at once.

While such headliners as Van Morrison, Bob Dylan, and Jimmy Buffett have drawn record-setting crowds in recent years, serious Jazz Fest aficionados savor the lesser-known acts. They range from Mardi Gras Indians to old-time bluesmen who have never played outside the Delta, from Dixieland to avant-garde, from African artists making rare U.S. appearances to the top names in Cajun, zydeco, and, of course, jazz.

Gone are the days when the event was held in Congo Square and only a few hundred people came. Now filling the infield of the Fair Grounds horse racing track up near City Park, the festival (which covers the last weekend in April and the first in May) is set up about as well as such an event can be. When the crowds get big, though—the second Saturday traditionally is the busiest—it can be tough to move around, especially if the grounds are muddy from rain. And the lines at the most popular of the several dozen food booths can be frustratingly long. However, the crowds are remarkably well behaved—to make a sweeping generalization, these are not the same types who come for Mardi Gras. Tellingly, there are few, if any, arrests during Jazz Fest.

Attending Jazz Fest means making a few decisions. Hotel and restaurant reservations, not to mention choice plane flights, fill up months (if not a year) in advance, but the schedule is not announced until a couple of months before the event. That may mean scheduling your visit around your own availability, not an appearance by a particular band. Just about every day at Jazz Fest is a good day, so this is not a hardship.

Whenever you decide to go, contact the **New Orleans Jazz and Heritage Festival,** 1205 N. Rampart St., New Orleans, LA 70116 (☎ **504/522-4786;** www.nojazzfest.com), to get the schedule for each weekend and information about other Jazz Fest–related shows around town.

Try to purchase tickets as early as February if possible. They're available by mail through **Ticketmaster** (☎ **504/522-5555**). To order tickets by phone, or to get ticket information, call **the Heritage Festival** (☎ **800/488-5252** outside Louisiana, or 504/522-5555; fax 504/379-3291). Admission for adults is $12 in advance and $16 at the gate; for children, $1.50 in advance and $2 at the gate. Evening events and concerts (order tickets in advance for these events as well) may be attended at an additional cost—usually between $20 and $30, depending on the concert.

JAZZ FEST PARKING & TRANSPORTATION   Parking at the Fair Grounds is next to impossible. We strongly recommend that you take public transportation or one of the available shuttles.

The **Regional Transit Authority** operates bus routes from various pickup points to the Fair Grounds. For schedules and information, call ☎ **504/248-3900.** Taxis, though probably scarce, will also take you to the Fair Grounds at a special event rate of $3 per person (or the meter reading if it's higher). We recommend **United Cabs** (☎ **504/524-9606**). The New Orleans Jazz and Heritage Festival provides information about shuttle transportation, which is not included in the ticket price.

PACKAGE DEALS   If you want to go to Jazz Fest but would rather someone else did all the planning, consider contacting **Festival Tours International** (15237 Sunset Blvd., Suite 17, Pacific Palisades, CA 90272; ☎ **310/454-4080;** e-mail: Festtours@

aol.com). Packages include not just accommodations and tickets for Jazz Fest, but also a visit to Cajun country for unique personal encounters with some of the finest local musicians.

If you're flying to New Orleans specifically for the Jazz and Heritage Festival, consider calling **Continental Airlines** (☎ **800/ 525-0280** or 504/581-2965). It's the official airline of Jazz Fest, and offers special fares during the event. You'll need the Jazz Fest promotional code, available from the festival's information line.

3   Other Top Festivals

SPRING FIESTA

The annual 5-day Spring Fiesta has been going on since 1935 and is a good opportunity to see the inside of some lovely old homes that are ordinarily closed to the public. Hostesses in antebellum dress escort you through the premises and provide all sorts of information and anecdotes. In the French Quarter, there are balcony concerts by sopranos. Out on River Road, there are plantation home tours. One highlight is the gala "Night in Old New Orleans" parade, which features carriages bearing passengers dressed as prominent figures in the city's history, as well as some of the best marching bands in town.

Spring Fiesta usually takes place over a full week in April. For full details, reservations, and a schedule of admission fees for some of the homes (around $15 for city tours, $45 for country estate tours), write to the **Spring Fiesta Association,** 826 St. Ann St., New Orleans, LA 70116 (☎ **504/581-1367**). You can order tickets by mail, or purchase them at the French Market Gift Shop, 824 Decatur St., and at Gray Line Tour Desks. For a list of locations, contact the Spring Fiesta Association.

TENNESSEE WILLIAMS FESTIVAL

In late March or early April, New Orleans honors one of its most illustrious writers. Although he was not born here, Tennessee Williams once said, "If I can be considered to have a home, it would have to be New Orleans . . . which has provided me with more material than any other city."

During the 3-day Tennessee Williams/New Orleans Literary Festival, many of his plays are performed, and there are symposiums and panel discussions on his work, as well as walking tours of his favorite French Quarter haunts. Other New Orleans–associated authors are celebrated as well (in fact, Williams has been somewhat deemphasized in recent years.)

For dates and details, contact festival organizers at 5500 Prytania St., Suite 217, New Orleans, LA 70115 (☎ **504/581-1144;** e-mail: twfest@gnofn.org).

FRENCH QUARTER FESTIVAL

The 3-day French Quarter Festival in early April is a celebration of the ingredients of French Quarter life. There are scores of free outdoor concerts, patio tours, a parade, a battle of jazz bands, art shows, children's activities, and talent and bartender competitions. As if that weren't enough, Jackson Square is transformed into the world's largest jazz brunch, with about 40 leading restaurants serving Cajun and Creole specialties such as jambalaya, gumbo, and crawfish fettuccine. Jazz aficionados are finding this festival somewhat more to their liking than Jazz Fest—despite the names, the Quarter Festival emphasizes that kind of music more.

For exact dates and other information, write to **French Quarter Festivals,** 100 Conti St., New Orleans, LA 70130 (☎ **504/522-5730**).

CREOLE CHRISTMAS

Leave it to New Orleans! A few days simply are not enough for this lively city to celebrate Christmas, so the entire month of December is designated "Creole Christmas." All sorts of gala events are sprinkled throughout the calendar, including tours of 19th-century homes decorated for the holidays, candlelight caroling in Jackson Square, cooking demonstrations, a madrigal dinner, gingerbread house demonstrations, and special Reveillon menus at select French Quarter restaurants. Hotels offer special "Papa No'l" rates from December 5 through December 25.

For full details, contact **French Quarter Festivals,** 100 Conti St., New Orleans, LA 70130 (☎ **504/522-5730**).

3

Getting to Know New Orleans

*N*ew Orleans is a very user-friendly city—that is, except for the un-usual directions and the nearly impossible-to-pronounce street names. It's a manageable size (only about 7 miles long) with most of what the average tourist would want to see concentrated in a few areas. This chapter contains some of the ins and outs of New Orleans navigation, and gives you some local sources to contact for special-ized information.

1 Orientation

ARRIVING

From the airport, you can reach the **Central Business District** by bus for $1.50 (exact change required). Buses run from 6am to 6:30pm. From 6 to 9am and 3 to 6pm, they leave the airport every 12 to 15 minutes and go to the downtown side of Tulane Avenue between Elks Place and South Saratoga Street; at other times, they leave every 23 minutes. For more information, call the **Louisiana Transit Company** (☎ 504/737-9611).

You can also get to your hotel on the **Airport Shuttle** (☎ 504/522-3500). For $10 per person (one way), the van will take you di-rectly to your hotel. There are Airport Shuttle information desks (staffed 24 hours) in the airport.

A **taxi** from the airport will cost about $21; if there are three or more passengers, the fare is $8 per person.

VISITOR INFORMATION

The **New Orleans Metropolitan Convention and Visitors Bureau,** 1520 Sugar Bowl Dr., New Orleans, LA 70112 (☎ 504/566-5055; www.nawlins.com; e-mail: tourism@nawlins.com), is one of the most helpful tourist centers in any major city. The incredibly friendly and helpful staff can answer almost any random question you may have.

Once you've arrived in the city, you also might want to stop by the **Visitor Information Center,** 529 St. Ann St. (☎ 504/566-5031), in the French Quarter. The center is open daily 9am to

5pm and has walking- and driving-tour maps and booklets on restaurants, accommodations, sightseeing, special tours, and pretty much anything else you might want to know about. You also might keep an eye out for the mobile **Info a la Cart** sites around town.

CITY LAYOUT

"Where y'at?" goes the traditional local greeting. "Where" is easy enough when you are in the French Quarter, the site of the original settlement. A 13-block-long grid between Canal Street and Esplanade Avenue, running from the Mississippi River to North Rampart Street, it's the closest the city comes to a geographic center.

After that, all bets are off. Because of the bend in the river, the streets are laid out at angles and curves that render north, south, east, and west useless. It's time to readjust your thinking: In New Orleans, the compass points are *riverside, lakeside, uptown,* and *downtown.* You'll catch on quickly if you keep in mind that North Rampart Street is the *lakeside* boundary of the Quarter, and that St. Charles Avenue extends from the French Quarter, *downtown,* to Tulane University, *uptown.*

Canal Street forms the boundary between new and old New Orleans. Street names change when they cross Canal (Bourbon Street, for example, becomes Carondelet Street), and addresses begin at 100 on either side of Canal. In the Quarter, street numbers begin at 400 at the river because 4 blocks of numbered buildings were lost to the river before the levee was built).

MAPS   Don't think you can get along without one in New Orleans! Call the Convention and Visitors Bureau (see above) or stop by the Visitor Information Center for a free one, or pay for one at any major bookstore. If you rent a car, be sure to ask for maps of the city—the rental agents have good ones. If you're planning excursions outside the city, the places listed above also supply state maps.

STREET NAMES   As if the streets themselves weren't colorful enough, there are the street names, from Felicity to the jaw-breaker Tchoupitoulas (say chop-i-*too*-las). How did they get these fanciful monikers? Well, in some cases, from overeducated city fathers, who named streets after Greek muses (Calliope and Terpsichore). Some immortalize long-dead and otherwise forgotten women: Julia was a free woman of color, but who was Felicity? Many streets in the French Quarter—Burgundy, Dauphine, Toulouse, and Dumaine—honor French royalty or nobility, while St. Peter and St. Ann were favorite baptismal names of the Orleans family. The Faubourg Marigny (Faubourg being the local word for *suburb*) was once part of the Marigny (say *Mare-i-nee*) family plantation. After scion Bernard squandered his family's fortune (mostly on gambling), he sold off parcels to the city, naming the streets after his favorite things: Desire, Piety, Poets, Duels, Craps, and so forth.

NEIGHBORHOODS IN BRIEF

The French Quarter Made up of about 90 square blocks, this section is also known as the *Vieux Carré* ("Old Square") and is enclosed by Canal Street, North Rampart Street, the Mississippi River, and Esplanade Avenue. The Quarter is full of commercial establishments, residences, and museums; its major public area is Jackson Square, bounded by Chartres, Decatur, St. Peter, and St. Ann streets. The most historic and best-preserved area in the city, it's likely to be the focal point of your stay.

Esplanade Ridge (Mid City) Stretching from the French Quarter to City Park, the Ridge hugs either side of Esplanade Avenue. This area encompasses a few distinct neighborhoods, all of which have certain things in common. In the 19th century, Esplanade was the grand avenue of New Orleans Creole society—the St. Charles Avenue of downriver. Many sections of the avenue and houses along it have seen better days, but there is still evidence of those times, especially in the ancient oak trees forming a canopy above the road.

The oldest section of Esplanade Ridge, **Faubourg Tremé,** is located directly across Rampart Street from the French Quarter. Like the Quarter, it was a dense 19th-century Creole community. Unlike the Quarter, Tremé has remained almost untouched by preservationists and so has continued to be an organic residential community. Today, it is one of the most vibrant African American neighborhoods in New Orleans, home to more than a few of the city's best brass bands. Unfortunately, Tremé is also plagued by severe crime, so it's not advisable to walk through at night.

Canal Street/Central Business District Historically, Canal Street has been New Orleans' main street, and in the 19th century it also divided the French and American sections of the city. (By the way, there's no canal—the one that was planned for the spot never came off.)

The **Central Business District (CBD)** is roughly bounded by Canal Street and the elevated Pontchartrain Expressway (Business

Route U.S. 90), between Loyola Avenue and the Mississippi River. Some of the most elegant luxury hotels are in this area. Most of the district was known as Faubourg St. Mary when Americans began settling here after the Louisiana Purchase. Lafayette Square was the center of life here during the 19th century.

Within the CBD is the **Warehouse District.** Twenty years ago, this area was full of abandoned warehouses and almost nothing else. With the efforts of some dedicated individuals and institutions, however, it's steadily evolving into a residential neighborhood with some commercial activity. Furthermore, this area also serves as the city's art gallery district, with most of the premier galleries concentrated along **Julia Street.** Most of these show the works of local and regional contemporary artists. The Contemporary Arts Center and Louisiana Children's Museum (see chapter 6) are also in this area.

Uptown/The Garden District   Bounded by St. Charles Avenue (lakeside) and Magazine Street (riverside) between Jackson and Louisiana avenues, the Garden District remains one of the most picturesque areas in the city. Originally the site of a plantation, the area was subdivided and developed as a residential neighborhood for wealthy Americans. Throughout the middle of the 19th century, developers built the Victorian, Italianate, and Greek Revival homes that still line the streets. Most of the homes had elaborate lawns and gardens, but few of those still exist.

The Irish Channel   The area bounded by Magazine Street and the Mississippi River, Louisiana Avenue, and the Central Business District got its name during the 1800s, when more than 100,000 Irish immigrated to New Orleans. As was true elsewhere in the country, the Irish of New Orleans were often considered "expendable" labor. Many were killed while employed at dangerous construction work and other manual labor. These days, the Channel is significantly less Irish, but it retains its lively spirit and distinctive neighborhood flavor. Much of the area is run-down, but just as much is filled with quiet residential neighborhoods. To get a glimpse of the Irish Channel, go to the antique shop district on Magazine Street and stroll between Felicity Street and Jackson Avenue.

Basin Street   You remember Basin Street, of course—it's the birthplace of jazz. Or at least that's the legend. In fact, jazz probably predates the rise of **Storyville** (the old red-light district along Basin Street), where it is said to have been born, by a good number of years. To give credit where credit is due, Storyville's "sporting

The City at a Glance

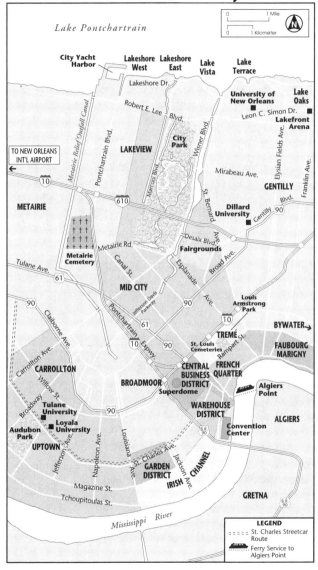

houses" did provide a place for the music to grab the ear of a wide segment of the public, who came to enjoy the houses', uh, services. King Oliver, Jelly Roll Morton, and Louis Armstrong were among the jazz greats who got their start on Basin Street in the brothels between Canal Street and Beauregard Square.

Apart from a couple of nondescript buildings, no trace of the old Storyville survives. A low-income public housing project now sprawls over much of the site, and statues depicting Latin American heroes—Simón Bolívar, Benito Juárez, and Gen. Francisco Morazán—dot the landscape.

Faubourg Marigny   *Faubourg* means "suburb," and *Marigny* is the name of a prominent early New Orleans family. This area is between the French Quarter (along Esplanade Avenue) and Bywater (along Press Street). Over the past decade, the Marigny has emerged as one of the city's vital centers of activity. You can still find the outlines of a small Creole suburb, and many old-time residents remain. Younger urban dwellers have moved into the area in significant numbers recently. Today, some of the best bars and nightspots in New Orleans are along Frenchmen Street, the Marigny's main drag. Along with the adjacent sections of the French Quarter, the Marigny is also a social center for the city's gay and lesbian communities.

Algiers Point   Directly across the Mississippi River from the Central Business District and the French Quarter, and connected by the Canal Street Ferry, the point is the old town center of Algiers. It is another of New Orleans' original Creole suburbs, but probably the one that has changed the least over the decades. Today, you can't see many signs of the area's once-booming railroad and dry-docking industries, but you can see some of the best-preserved small gingerbread and Creole cottages in New Orleans.

Bywater   This riverside neighborhood is past the Faubourg Marigny and bounded on the east by an industrial canal. At first glance it seems like a wasteland of light industry and run-down homes. In fact, Bywater has plenty of nice, modest residential sections. Furthermore, it's home to the city's artists-in-hiding, and many local designers have shops among the urban decay.

SAFETY

The city's high crime rate has made headlines over the past few years. New Orleans has worked hard on the problem, and an increased police force and vigilance have led to a decrease in crime.

However, problems still remain, and we want to help you avoid them as best you can. We consulted with the Convention and Visitors Bureau and a 7-year member of the New Orleans Police Department, and have these tips to offer. Mostly, it's a matter of relying on common sense and taking a few precautions.

STREET SMARTS The **French Quarter** is fairly safe, thanks to the number of people present at any given time, but some areas are better than others. On **Bourbon Street,** be careful when socializing with strangers, and be alert to distractions by potential pickpocket teams. Dauphine and Burgundy streets are in quiet, lovely old parts of the Quarter, but as you near Esplanade, watch out for purse snatchers. At night, stay in lighted areas with street and pedestrian traffic, and take cabs down Esplanade Avenue and into the **Faubourg Marigny.** Do not walk alone much past Bourbon toward Rampart after dark. Stay in a group or see if you can get a beat cop to escort you. In the **Garden District,** as you get past Magazine toward the river, the neighborhoods can be rough, so exercise caution.

At all times, try to avoid looking distracted or confused. If you appear confident and alert, you will look less like a target.

TRAVEL SMARTS Don't hang that expensive camera around your neck when it's not in use. Put it out of sight, if you can, in a camera bag or other case. If the bag or case has a shoulder strap, carry it so the bag is on your hip with strap over the opposite shoulder, so a simple tug won't dislodge it. That goes for purses as well. You might consider using a money belt or other hidden, pickpocket-proof type of travel wallet. (Women probably won't want to bring purses to clubs where they plan on dancing.) And never leave valuables in the outside pocket of a backpack. Should you stop for a bite to eat, keep everything within easy reach. If you're traveling in a car, place your belongings in the trunk, not under the seat. And it's always a good idea to leave expensive-looking jewelry and other conspicuous valuables at home, anyway.

2 Getting Around

You really don't need to rent a car during your stay. Not only is the town just made for walking (thanks to being so flat—and so darn picturesque), but most places you want to go are easily accessible on foot or by some form of the largely excellent public transportation system. Indeed, we find a streetcar ride as much entertainment as practical means of getting around. At night, when you need them most, cabs are easy to come by.

BY PUBLIC TRANSPORTATION

DISCOUNT PASSES   If you won't have a car in New Orleans, we strongly encourage you to invest in a **VisiTour** pass, which entitles you to an unlimited number of rides on all streetcar and bus lines. It costs $4 for 1 day, $8 for 3 days. Passes are available from VisiTour vendors—to find the nearest one, ask at your hotel or guest house or call **the Regional Transit Authority** (☎ **504/248-3900**). You can call the RTA for information about any part of the city's public transportation system.

BUSES   New Orleans has an excellent public bus system, so chances are there's a bus that runs exactly where you want to go. Local fares at press time are $1 (you must have exact change, in bills or coins), transfers are an extra 10¢, and express buses are $1.25. You can get complete route information by calling the RTA (☎ **504/ 248-3900**) or by picking up one of the excellent city maps available at the Visitor Information Center, 529 St. Ann St. (☎ **504/ 568-5661**), in the French Quarter.

STREETCARS   Besides being a national historic landmark, the **St. Charles Avenue streetcar** is also a convenient and fun way to get from downtown to Uptown and back. The trolleys run 24 hours a day at frequent intervals, and the fare is $1 each way (you must have exact change in bills or coins).

The streetcar line extends beyond the point where St. Charles Avenue bends into Carrollton Avenue. The end of the line is at Palmer Park and Playground at Clairborne Avenue, but you'll want to mount a shopping expedition at the Riverbend Shopping Area (see chapter 7). It will cost you another $1 for the ride back to Canal Street. It costs 10¢ to transfer from the streetcar to a bus.

The **riverfront streetcar** runs for 1.9 miles, from the Old Mint across Canal Street to Riverview, with stops along the way. It's a great step-saver as you explore the riverfront. The fare is $1.25, and there's ramp access.

BY CAR

If you absolutely have to have a car, try one of the following car-rental agencies: **Avis,** 2024 Canal St. (☎ **800/331-1212** or 504/ 523-4317); **Budget Rent-A-Car,** 1317 Canal St. (☎ **800/527-0700** or 504/467-2277); **Dollar Rent-A-Car,** 1910 Airline Hwy., Kenner (☎ **800/800-4000** or 504/467-2285); **Hertz,** 901 Convention Center Blvd., No. 101 (☎ **800/654-3131** or 504/568-1645);

Swifty Car Rental, 2300 Canal St. (☎ **504/524-7368**); **Value Rent-A-Car,** 1806 Airline Hwy., Kenner (☎ **800/GO-VALUE** or 504/469-2688).

Rental rates vary according to the time of your visit and from company to company, so call ahead and do some comparison shopping. Ask lots of questions, try different dates and pickup points, and ask about corporate or organizational discounts. And if you're staying for a week or more, be sure to ask about weekly rates, which are cheaper.

New Orleans drivers are often reckless, so drive defensively. The meter maids are an efficient bunch, so take no chances with parking meters. Carry change with you, as many meters take only quarters. It's probably best to use your car only for longer jaunts away from congested areas. Most hotels provide guest parking, often for a daily fee; smaller hotels or guest houses (particularly in the French Quarter) may not have parking facilities but will be able to direct you to a nearby public garage.

The narrow streets and frequent congestion make driving in the French Quarter more difficult than elsewhere in the city. The streets are one way, and on weekdays during daylight hours, Royal and Bourbon streets between the 300 and 700 blocks are closed to automobiles. Also, the blocks of Chartres Street in front of St. Louis Cathedral are closed at all times. Driving is also trying in the Central Business District, where congestion and limited parking make life difficult for the motorist. Do yourself a favor: Park the car and use public transportation in both areas.

Once you get into more residential areas, like the Garden District, and off main drags like St. Charles, finding where you are going becomes quite the challenge. Street signs are often no bigger than a postcard, and hard to read at that. At night, they aren't even lit, so deciphering where you are can be next to impossible. If you must drive, we suggest counting the number of streets you have to cross to tell you when to make any turns, rather than relying on street signs.

BY TAXI

Taxis are plentiful in New Orleans. They can be hailed easily on the street in the French Quarter and some parts of the Central Business District, and are usually lined up at taxi stands at larger hotels. Otherwise, telephone and expect a cab to appear in 3 to 5 minutes. The rate is $2.10 when you enter the taxi and $1.20 per mile thereafter. During special events (like Mardi Gras and Jazz Fest), the rate is $3 per person (or the meter rate if it's greater) no matter where you go in the city. The city's most reliable company is **United Cabs** (☎ **504/524-9606**).

ON FOOT

We can't stress this enough: Walking is by far the best way to see this town. There are too many unique and sometimes glorious sights to want to whiz past them. Slow down. Have a drink to go. Get a snack. Stroll. Sure, sometimes it's too darn hot or humid—or raining too darn hard—to make walking attractive, but there is always a cab or bus nearby. Do remember to drink lots of water if it's hot, and pay close attention to your surroundings. If you enter an area that seems unsafe, retreat.

BY FERRY

The Canal Street ferry is one of New Orleans' secrets—and it's free for pedestrians. The ride takes you across the Mississippi River from the foot of Canal to Algiers Point (25 minutes round-trip), and affords great views of downtown New Orleans and of the commerce on the river. Once in Algiers, you can walk around the old Algiers Point neighborhood. At night, with the city's glowing skyline reflecting on the river, a ride on the ferry can be quite romantic. The ferry also does carry car traffic, in case you'd like to do some West Bank driving.

FAST FACTS: New Orleans

Airport See "Getting There" in chapter 1, and "Orientation," earlier in this chapter.

American Express The local office (☎ **504/586-8201**) is at 158 Baronne St. in the Central Business District. It's open weekdays 9am to 5pm.

Area Code The area code for New Orleans is **504.**

Baby-sitters It's best to ask at your hotel about baby-sitting services. If your hotel doesn't offer help finding child care, try calling **Accent on Children's Arrangements** (☎ **504/524-1227**).

Emergencies For fire, ambulance, and police, dial ☎ **911.** This is a free call from pay phones.

Hospitals Should you become ill during your visit, most major hotels have in-house doctors on call 24 hours a day. If no one is available at your hotel or guest house, call or go to the emergency room at **Ochsner Medical Institutions,** 1516 Jefferson Hwy. (☎ 504/842-3460), or the **Tulane University Medical Center,** 1415 Tulane Ave. (☎ **504/588-5800**).

Information See "Visitor Information," earlier in this chapter.

Liquor Laws The legal drinking age in Louisiana is 21, but don't be surprised if people much younger take a seat next to you at the bar. Alcoholic beverages are available around the clock, 7 days a week. You're allowed to drink on the street, but not from a glass or bottle. Bars will often provide a plastic "go cup" so you can transfer your drink as you leave (and some have walk-up windows for quick and easy refills).

One warning: Although the police may look the other way if they see a pedestrian who's had a few too many (as long as he or she is peaceful and not bothering anyone), they have no tolerance at all for those who are intoxicated behind the wheel.

Maps See "City Layout," earlier in this chapter.

Newspapers & Magazines To find out what's going on around town, you might want to pick up a copy of the daily **Times-Picayune** or **Offbeat**—a monthly guide (probably the most extensive one available) to the city's evening entertainment, art galleries, and special events. It can be found in most hotels, though it's often hard to find toward the end of the month. The **Gambit Weekly** is the city's free alternative paper, and has a good mix of news and entertainment information. It comes out every Thursday.

Pharmacies The 24-hour pharmacy closest to the French Quarter is **Walgreens,** at 3311 Canal St., at Jefferson Davis (☎ **504/822-8072**).

Police Dial ☎ **911** for emergencies.

Post Office The main post office is at 701 Loyola Ave. There's also a post office in the World Trade Center. If you're in the Quarter, you'll find a post office at 1022 Iberville St. There's another one at 610 S. Maestri Place. If you have something large or fragile to send home and don't feel like hunting around for packing materials, go to **Prytania Mail Services,** 5500 Prytania St. (☎ **504/897-0877**), uptown.

Radio WWOZ FM 90.7 is *the* New Orleans radio station. They say they are the best in the world, and we aren't inclined to disagree. New Orleans jazz, R&B, brass bands, Mardi Gras Indians, gospel, Cajun, zydeco—it's all here.

Safety   Be careful while visiting any unfamiliar city. In New Orleans in particular, don't walk alone at night, and don't go into the cemeteries alone at any time during the day or night. Ask around locally before you go anywhere. People will tell you if you should take a cab instead of walking or using public transportation. Most important, if someone holds you up and demands your wallet, purse, or other personal belongings, don't resist.

Taxes   The **sales tax** in New Orleans is 9%. An additional 2% tax is added to hotel bills, for a total of 11%.

Time Zone   New Orleans observes central time, the same as Chicago. Between the first Sunday in April and the last Saturday in October, daylight saving time is in effect. During this period, clocks are set 1 hour ahead of standard time. Call ☎ **504/976-1111** for the correct local time.

Transit Information   Local bus routes and schedules can be obtained from the **RTA Ride Line** (☎ **504/248-3900**). **Union Passenger Terminal,** 1001 Loyola Ave., provides bus information (☎ **504/524-7571**) and train information (☎ **504/528-1610**).

Traveler's Aid Society   You can reach the local branch of the society at ☎ **504/525-8726.**

Weather   For an update, call ☎ **504/828-4000.**

4

Accommodations

*I*f you're doing your New Orleans trip right, you shouldn't be doing much sleeping. But you do have to put your change of clothes somewhere. New Orleans is bursting with hotels of every variety, so you should be able to find something that fits your preferences. However, during crowded times (Mardi Gras, for example), just finding anything might have to be good enough. After all, serious New Orleans visitors often book a year in advance for popular times. That's competition!

However, here are a few tips. Don't stay on Bourbon Street unless you absolutely have to, or don't mind getting no sleep. The open-air frat party that is this thoroughfare does mean a free show below your window, but is hardly conducive to . . . well, just about anything other than participation in same. If you must stay on Bourbon Street, try to get a room away from the street.

A first-time visitor might also strongly consider not staying in the Quarter at all. Most of your sightseeing will take place there, so why not try the beautiful **Garden District** instead? It's an easy streetcar ride away from the Quarter, and closer to a number of wonderful clubs and restaurants. Conventioneers and businesspeople tend to favor the **Central Business District**. It is closer to their kind of action, but has not produced much in the way of colorful hotels, and is a largely sterile location otherwise.

All of the guest houses in this chapter are first rate. If you want more information, we highly recommend the ✪ **Bed and Breakfast, Inc. Reservation Service,** 1021 Moss St. (P.O. Box 52257), New Orleans, LA 70152 (☎ **800/729-4640** or 504/488-4640).

As a general rule, just to be on the safe side, always book ahead during spring, fall, and winter. And if your trip will coincide with Mardi Gras or Jazz Fest, book way ahead—up to a year in advance, if you want to be sure of a room. Sugar Bowl week and other festival times when visitors flood New Orleans also require planning for accommodations, and there's always the chance that a big convention will be in town, making it difficult to find a room. You might conceivably run across a cancellation and get a last-minute booking,

New Orleans Accommodations

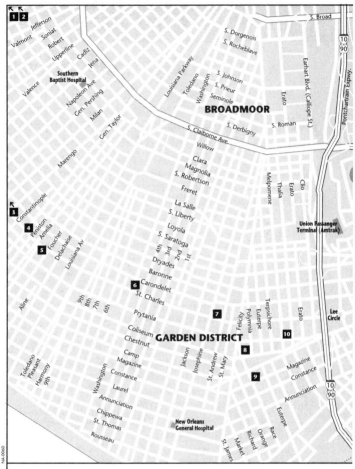

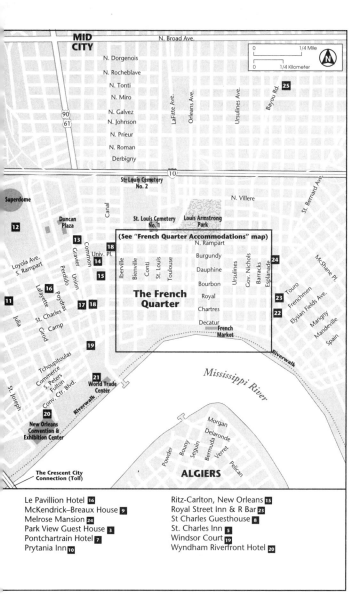

Le Pavillion Hotel **16**
McKendrick–Breaux House **9**
Melrose Mansion **24**
Park View Guest House **3**
Pontchartrain Hotel **7**
Prytania Inn **10**

Ritz-Carlton, New Orleans **15**
Royal Street Inn & R Bar **23**
St Charles Guesthouse **8**
St. Charles Inn **5**
Windsor Court **19**
Wyndham Riverfront Hotel **20**

but the chances are remote at best. You should also be aware that rates frequently jump more than a notch or two for Mardi Gras and other festival times (sometimes they even double), and in some cases there's a 4- or 5-night minimum requirement.

If you want to miss the crowds and the lodgings squeeze that mark the big festivals, consider coming in the month immediately following Mardi Gras, or, if you can stand the heat and humidity, in the summer, when the streets are not nearly as thronged. December, before the Sugar Bowl and New Year's activities, is a good time, too, but perhaps a bit rainy.

Rates are for double rooms and do not include the city's 11% hotel tax. Reduced single-occupancy rates are often offered; inquire when you make reservations. Unless otherwise noted, all accommodations in New Orleans have private bathrooms.

1 The French Quarter

VERY EXPENSIVE

✪ **Melrose Mansion.** 937 Esplanade Ave., New Orleans, LA 70116. ☎ **800/ 650-3323** or 504/944-2255. Fax 504/945-1794. 10 units. A/C MINIBAR TV TEL. $225–$250 double; $325–$425 suite. Rates include champagne breakfast and cocktail hour. AE, DISC, MC, V. Parking available on street.

Even on a street full of envy-inducing mansions, in a town full of pampering guest houses, the Melrose Mansion (and soon to be Spa) is an experience. Think luxury resort living, combined with the best of guest house offerings, and you should get the idea. A charming old mansion, beautifully renovated, is the setting, where full-time butlers, soft music, evening candles, and other touches combine for a rarified, but not snooty atmosphere. The rooms vary, from classic Victorian antiques to lighter country-style decor.

✪ **Omni Royal Orleans.** 621 St. Louis St., New Orleans, LA 70140. ☎ **800/ THE-OMNI** in the U.S. and Canada, or 504/529-5333. Fax 504/529-7089. www.omnihotel.com. 346 units. A/C MINIBAR TV TEL. $129–$309 double; $269–$649 suite; $949 penthouse. Children under 18 stay free in parents' room. AE, CB, DC, DISC, MC, V. Valet parking $15.

Despite being part of a chain, this is a most elegant hotel that, unlike others in its class, escapes feeling sterile and generic. This is only proper, given that it is on the former site of the venerable 1836 St. Louis Exchange Hotel, one of the country's premier hostelries and a center of New Orleans social life until the final years of the Civil War. The lobby is a small sea of marble and brass and crystal chandeliers. Furnishings in the guest rooms are equally elegant, full of muted tones and plush furniture, with windows that let you look dreamily out over the Quarter. Service varies between exceptional and slightly lacking when they are busy.

Dining: The classic Rib Room is a favorite dining spot for many natives, and there's soft music after 8pm in the sophisticated Esplanade Lounge. Touché Bar offers light meals and excellent mint juleps. The rooftop, poolside La Riviera bar and restaurant is a terrific lunch spot.

Amenities: Health club, heated outdoor pool, concierge, babysitting, emergency mending and pressing, complimentary shoe shine, 24-hour room service, beauty and barber shops, florist, sundries shop and newsstand, business center.

Ritz-Carlton, New Orleans. 921 Canal St., New Orleans, LA 70112. ☎ **800/ 241-3333** or 504/524-1331. 452 units. A/C MINIBAR TV TEL. $335 double. Suites $685 and way, way up. AE, DC, MC, V.

Sentimentalists that we are, we were deeply sad to see the venerable Maison Blanche department store go the way of Woolworth's, D. H. Holmes, and other Canal Street shopping landmarks. But for New Orleans' sake, we are pleased to have a Ritz-Carlton take its place. The hotel is due to open at the end of 1999, and should bring plenty of Ritz luxury.

Westin Canal Place. 100 Rue Iberville, New Orleans, LA 70130. ☎ **800/ 228-3000** or 504/566-7006. www.westin1.com. 437 units. A/C MINIBAR TV TEL. $289–$319 double. AE, CB, DC, DISC, MC, V. $15 valet parking, $13 self-parking.

At the foot of Canal Street, the Westin Canal Place is in the French Quarter, but not quite *of* it. It is, literally, *above* the Quarter: The grand-scale lobby, with its fine paintings and antiques, is on the 11th floor of the Canal Place tower. The guest rooms are on the floors above; each has a marble foyer and bathroom, fine furnishings (including particularly good pillows), and phones with call waiting and voice mail. Needless to say, this hotel provides some of the city's most expansive views of the river and the French Quarter.

Dining: The lobby makes an impressive setting for afternoon tea. The Green Bar and the Riverbend Grill restaurant are just steps away. There is also a Sunday jazz brunch.

Amenities: Heated pool, privileges at nearby 18-hole golf course, tour desk, concierge, 24-hour room service, multilingual staff, dry cleaning and laundry, newspaper delivery. There's direct elevator access to Canal Place shopping center, where guests can use the health center free of charge or visit the barber shop, beauty salon, and stores.

EXPENSIVE

Best Western Inn on Bourbon Street. 541 Bourbon St., New Orleans, LA 70130. ☎ **800/535-7891** or 504/524-7611. Fax 504/568-9427. www. innonbourbon.com. 186 units. A/C MINIBAR TV TEL. $195–$275 double. AE, CB, DC, DISC, MC, V. Valet parking $13.

Party animals and party animal–phobes should note this location is right in the middle of the liveliest action on Bourbon, and many rooms have balconies overlooking the mayhem below. If you have a serious commitment to sleeping, you might want to choose another place to stay, or at least request an interior room. All rooms have Deep South decor and king or double beds.

Dining: There's a lounge in the lobby. The Bourbon Street Cafeteria serves breakfast.

Amenities: Fitness room, outdoor pool, concierge, dry cleaning and laundry, newspaper delivery, baby-sitting by arrangement, express checkout, jewelry shop, gift shop.

Dauphine Orleans Hotel. 415 Dauphine St., New Orleans, LA 70112. ☎ **800/521-7111** or 504/586-1800. Fax 504/586-1409. www. dauphineorleans.com. 111 units. A/C MINIBAR TV TEL. $149–$199 double; $149–$259 patio room; $179–$359 suite. Rates include continental breakfast and afternoon tea. Extra person $15. Children under 17 stay free in parents' room. AE, CB, DC, DISC, MC, V. Valet parking $12.

On a relatively quiet and peaceful block of the Quarter, the Dauphine Orleans Hotel sports a casual elegance. It's just a block from the action on Bourbon Street, but you wouldn't know it if you were sitting in any of its three secluded courtyards. The hotel's buildings have a colorful history. The license a former owner took out to make the place a bordello is proudly displayed in the bar, and its proprietors are happy to admit that ghosts have been sighted on the premises. All rooms have recently been upgraded with marble bathrooms and new furnishings, either modern or upgraded period pieces.

Dining: May Baily's, the hotel bar, was once a notorious "sporting house" (brothel). Breakfast is served from 6:30 to 11am in the Coffee Lounge. Afternoon tea is served daily from 3 to 5pm.

Amenities: Outdoor pool, small fitness room, concierge, dry cleaning and laundry, baby-sitting, complimentary French Quarter and downtown transportation, newspaper delivery, guest library, Jacuzzi.

✪ **Hotel Maison de Ville.** 727 Toulouse St., New Orleans, LA 70130. ☎ **800/634-1600** or 504/561-5858. Fax 504/528-9939. www. maisondeville.com. 23 units, 5 cottages. A/C MINIBAR TV TEL. $195–$225 double; $215–$235 queen; $225–$245 king; $325–$375 suite; $235–$325 1-bedroom cottage; $535–$725 2-bedroom cottage; $770–$1,005 3-bedroom cottage. AE, DC, MC, V. Valet parking $18.

French Quarter Accommodations

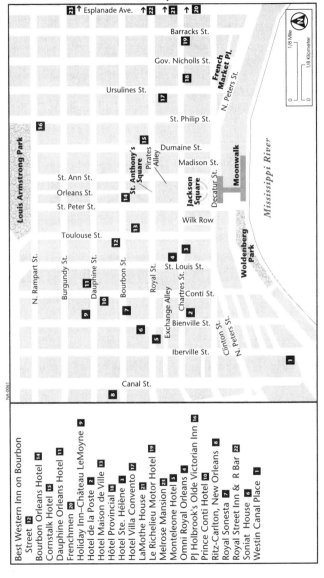

Best Western Inn on Bourbon Street **12**
Bourbon Orleans Hotel **14**
Cornstalk Hotel **15**
Dauphine Orleans Hotel **11**
Frenchmen **20**
Holiday Inn–Château LeMoyne **9**
Hotel de la Poste **2**
Hotel Maison de Ville **13**
Hôtel Provincial **18**
Hotel Ste. Hélène **3**
Hotel Villa Convento **17**
LaMothe House **21**
Le Richelieu Motor Hotel **19**
Melrose Mansion **23**
Monteleone Hotel **5**
Omni Royal Orleans **4**
PJ Holbrook's Olde Victorian Inn **16**
Prince Conti Hotel **10**
Ritz-Carlton, New Orleans **8**
Royal Sonesta **7**
Royal Street Inn & R Bar **22**
Soniat House **6**
Westin Canal Place **1**

43

On the list of Best Small Hotels in the World, the Maison de Ville is a great splurge. Tennessee Williams was a regular guest in room no. 9. Most of the rooms surround an utterly charming courtyard (complete with fountain and banana trees), where it's hard to imagine you're in the thick of the Quarter. The hotel is elegant and antique-filled. Rooms vary dramatically in size; some can be downright tiny, so ask when you reserve, as price is no indicator of size. All accommodations are thoroughly lush, with nice touches like featherbeds, and the service is stupendous. A great romantic getaway.

Dining: Continental breakfast is served in your room, in the parlor, or on the patio. Complimentary sherry and port are served in the afternoon and evening. Le Bistro, the hotel's restaurant, is intimate and inviting.

Amenities: Outdoor pool, access to nearby health club, concierge, room service (7am to 10pm), twice-daily maid service, newspaper delivery, shoe shine, dry cleaning and laundry.

Monteleone Hotel. 214 Royal St., New Orleans, LA 70130. ☎ **800/ 535-9595** or 504/523-3341. Fax 504/528-1019. www.hotelmonteleone.com. 600 units. A/C TV TEL. $140–$225 double or king double; $360–$900 suite. Extra person $25. Children under 18 stay free in parents' room. Package rates available. AE, CB, DC, DISC, MC, V. Valet parking $13 car, $17 van.

Opened in 1886, the Monteleone is the oldest hotel in the city. It's also the largest hotel in the French Quarter, and seems to keep getting bigger without losing a trace of its trademark charm. The Monteleone is defined by its lobby, made irresistibly grand by a delicately painted ceiling, chandeliers, and a marble floor. Service is surprisingly personal. Accommodations range in style from luxurious, antique-filled suites to more modern, comfortable family rooms.

Dining/Diversions: Le Café restaurant is a favorite with New Orleans natives; even if you stay elsewhere, stop by to see the revolving Carousel Bar.

Amenities: Heated rooftop swimming pool (open year-round), hot tub, sauna, fitness center, concierge, room service 6am to 11pm, laundry, baby-sitting.

✪ **Royal Sonesta.** 300 Bourbon St., New Orleans, LA 70140. ☎ **800/ 766-3782** or 504/586-0300. Fax 504/586-0335. www.royalsonestano.com. 500 units. A/C MINIBAR TV TEL. $205–$340 double; $400–$1,400 suite. AE, CB, DC, DISC, MC, V. Parking $15.

This is the most upscale hotel in the French Quarter. The contrast between the hurlyburly of Bourbon Street and the Sonesta's marbled and chandeliered lobby and its inner courtyard couldn't be greater. Some people consider this the only acceptable, top-flight Bourbon Street hotel, though noise is still a problem in rooms that face Bourbon (or even the side streets).

Dining/Diversions: Desire offers fresh seafood and an oyster bar. The Can Can Cafe features live Dixieland jazz.

Amenities: Room service until 2am, exercise room, business center.

✪ **Soniat House.** 1133 Chartres St., New Orleans, LA 70116. ☎ **800/544-8808** or 504/522-0570. Fax 504/522-7208. 33 units. A/C TV TEL. $165–$245 double; $295–$495 suite; $625 2-bedroom suite. AE, MC, V. Valet parking $16.

The recipient of a seemingly endless series of tributes from various prestigious travel journals, the Soniat House lives up to the hype. Keeping a low profile behind a solid wood gate, it's classic Creole, where the treasures are hidden off the street. The beyond-efficient staff will spoil you and the sweet courtyards, candlelit at night, will soothe you. Rooms do vary, if not in quality, then at least in distinction. Children over 12 are welcome only in rooms that accommodate three.

Dining: The "Southern Continental" breakfast, available every morning after 7am, costs $7 extra, but it's worth it. There is a fully stocked honor bar in the parlor next to the reception area.

Amenities: Jacuzzi, access to nearby health club and business center (for an additional charge), concierge, same-day dry-cleaning and laundry, newspaper delivery.

MODERATE

✪ **Bourbon Orleans Hotel.** 717 Orleans St., New Orleans, LA 70116. ☎ **504/523-2222.** Fax 504/525-8166. 216 units. A/C MINIBAR TV TEL. $119–$189 petite queen or twin; $139–$209 deluxe king or double; $179–$249 junior suite; $229–$379 town house suite; $259–$459 town house suite with balcony. Extra person $20. AE, CB, DC, DISC, MC, V. Valet parking $14.55.

The Bourbon Orleans takes up an entire block of prime real estate at the intersection of—guess where—Bourbon and Orleans streets. Public spaces are lavishly decorated but their elegant interest doesn't quite extend to the guest rooms. Bigger than average, they will give no cause for complaint about either decor (standard for this area, though even after upgrades, rooms feel tired rather than fresh and exciting) or comfort (we do like the Bath & Bodyworks amenities) but you can't help but want something a little more striking. There's a good-sized pool on the premises. The elegant lobby bar features a nightly cocktail hour.

Cornstalk Hotel. 915 Royal St., New Orleans, LA. 70116. ☎ **504/523-1515.** Fax 504/522-5558. 14 units. A/C TV TEL. Summer $75–$155 double; winter $135–$175 double. Rates include continental breakfast. AE, MC, V. Parking $5.

Thanks to the famous fence out front, this might be better known as a sightseeing stop for tourists than a place to stay. A gorgeous Victorian home on the National Register of Historic Places, it's nearly as pretty inside as out. The location couldn't be better. The requisite antiques dominate; if you are looking for period charm, look no further. The high-ceilinged rooms have fireplaces or stained-glass windows, and some have plasterwork (ceiling medallions, scrolls, and cherubs) from old plantations. The large front gallery, set unusually far back from the street, and the upstairs balcony provide perfect spots for sipping coffee in the morning or sherry after a hard day's shopping.

✪ **The Frenchmen.** 417 Frenchmen St., New Orleans, LA 70116. ☎ **800/ 831-1781** or 504/948-2166. Fax 504/948-2258. www.french-quarter.org. 27 units. A/C TV TEL. $79–$155 double. Rates include breakfast. AE, DISC, MC, V. Free parking.

This small, sweet, and slightly funky inn is very popular with in-the-know regular visitors. It's not for some, but others become loyal repeat customers. At the intersection of Esplanade Avenue and Frenchmen Street, it's just across from the Quarter and a block away from the main drag of the Frenchmen section of the Faubourg Marigny, where there are all sorts of clubs and happenings at night. Housed in two 19th-century buildings that were once grand New Orleans homes, the rooms are each individually decorated and furnished with antiques. They vary in size considerably, however, and some are very small indeed. Standard rooms have one double bed, some rooms have private balconies, and others have a loft bedroom with a sitting area.

Holiday Inn–Château LeMoyne. 301 Dauphine St., New Orleans, LA 70112. ☎ **800/HOLIDAY** or 504/581-1303. Fax 504/523-5709. 171 units. A/C TV TEL. $159–$244 double; $259–$459 suite. Extra person $15. AE, CB, DC, DISC, MC, V. Valet parking $17.

It's a nice surprise to find a Holiday Inn housed in century-plus old buildings, but the ambience stops at your room's threshold. Once inside, matters look pretty much like they do in every Holiday Inn. One of these 19th-century buildings was by famed architect James Gallier, and you can still see bits of old brick, old ovens, and exposed cypress beams here and there, along with a graceful curving outdoor staircase.

Hotel de la Poste. 316 Chartres St., New Orleans, LA 70130. ☎ **800/448-4927** or 504/581-1200. Fax 504/523-2910. 100 units. A/C TV TEL. $109–$229 standard double; $134–$254 deluxe double; $279 suite. Children under 16 stay free in parents' room. AAA and senior discounts available. AE, CB, DC, DISC, MC, V. Valet parking $18.

The nonbusiness crowd looking for a small family hotel is usually pleased with the Hotel de la Poste. Accommodations are mostly spacious (including big dressing areas and closets), though rooms with king-sized beds lose much of their floor space to same. The courtyard is a fine gathering spot, with piped-in music and a small unheated pool. Unfortunately, it shares boundaries with the parking garage driveway. *USA Today* is delivered to your room; your phone will feature voice mail and a data port; and you'll get a hair dryer, iron, and ironing board. Complimentary coffee, tea, and apples are available 24 hours a day.

Hôtel Provincial. 1024 Chartres St., New Orleans, LA 70116. ☎ **800/535-7922** or 504/581-4995. Fax 504/581-1018. www.hotelprovincial.com. 100 units. A/C TV TEL. $119–$289 double. Summer packages available. AE, CB, DC, DISC, MC, V. Valet parking $11.

Don't mention this to the owners, who are sensitive about it, but word from the ghost tours is that the Provincial is haunted. It must not be too much of a problem, because guests rave about the hotel and never mention ghostly visitors. With flickering gas lamps, no elevators, no fewer than five patios, and an overall tranquil setting, this feels less like a hotel than a guest house. It's also in a good part of the Quarter, on a quiet street off the beaten path. Rooms have high ceilings and all have at least a few antiques.

✪ **Hotel Ste. Hélène.** 508 Chartres St., New Orleans, LA 70130. ☎ **800/348-3888** or 504/522-5014. Fax 504/523-7140. www.stehelene.com. 26 units. A/C TV TEL. $125–$185 double. Rates include continental breakfast and champagne 5:30–6:30pm. AE, CB, DC, DISC, JCB, MC, V. Parking (about $10) in nearby lot.

In our opinion, this is what a slightly funky Quarter hotel should be. What it lacks in magnificence, it makes up for in character and location (less than two blocks from Jackson Square, in the heart of the Quarter). Rooms vary in size and style; front rooms have balconies overlooking the street, others have beds set in alcoves (we find it romantic, though you might find it claustrophobic) with a sort of low-rent parlor sitting area. The property winds about several buildings, with surprises at every turn. Throughout are interior and exterior courtyards, some with flickering gas lamps.

Hotel Villa Convento. 616 Ursulines St., New Orleans, LA 70116. ☎ **504/ 522-1793.** Fax 504/524-1902. www.neworleansonline.com/convento.htm. 25 units. A/C TV TEL. $89–$125 double; $155 suite. Rates include continental breakfast. Extra person $10. AE, CB, DC, DISC, MC, V. Parking $12.

Local tour guides say this was the original House of the Rising Sun bordello. With its rather small public spaces and the personal attention that its owners and operators, the Campo family, give to their guests, the Villa Convento has the feel of a small European inn or guest house. The building is a Creole town house; some rooms open onto the tropical patio, others to the street, and many have balconies.

✪ **LaMothe House.** 621 Esplanade Ave., New Orleans, LA 70116. ☎ **800/ 367-5858** or 504/947-1161. Fax 504/943-6536. www.new-orleans.org. 20 units. A/C TV TEL. $64–$275 double. Rates include breakfast. AE, DISC, MC, V. Free parking.

Somehow, a shiny new hotel doesn't seem quite right for New Orleans. More appropriate is slightly faded, somewhat threadbare elegance. The LaMothe House neatly fits that bill. The Creole-style plain facade of the 1840s town house a mossy, brick-lined courtyard with a fish-filled fountain and banana trees, and rooms filled with antiques that are worn in the right places, but not shabby. It's a short walk to the action in the Quarter and just a couple of blocks to the bustling Frenchmen scene.

Le Richelieu Motor Hotel. 1234 Chartres St., New Orleans, LA 70116. ☎ **800/535-9653** or 504/529-2492. Fax 504/524-8179. 86 units. A/C MINIBAR TV TEL. $95–$170 double; $170–$475 suite. Extra person or child $15. French Quarter Explorer and honeymoon packages available. AE, CB, DC, DISC, JCB, MC, V. Free parking.

First a row mansion, then a macaroni factory, and now a hotel, this building has seen it all. It's at the Esplanade edge of the Quarter— a perfect spot from which to explore the Faubourg Marigny. Though slightly run-down these days, it's good for families. Rooms are standard high-end motel rooms; many have balconies, and all overlook either the French Quarter or the courtyard.

✪ **P. J. Holbrook's Olde Victorian Inn.** 914 N. Rampart St., New Orleans, LA 70116. ☎ **800/725-2446** or 504/522-2446. Fax 504/897-0248. 6 units. A/C. $120–$175 double. Rates include full breakfast. Senior discount and weekly rates available. AE, MC, V. Parking available on street.

Walking into P. J.'s is like walking through time. The entire house is done in Victorian style, from the "gathering room" to the dining room. P. J. has gone to the ends of the earth to find the perfect pieces, draperies, color schemes, and curios. Most of the thoughtfully decorated rooms have fireplaces, and one even has a balcony set over North Rampart. A couple of units' private bathrooms are across the hall. P. J. herself is a most gracious host who will look after your every need.

Prince Conti Hotel. 830 Conti St., New Orleans, LA 70112. ☎ **800/366-2743** or 504/529-4172. Fax 504/581-3802. 53 units. A/C TV TEL. $120–$175 double; $195–$215 suite. AE, DC, DISC, MC, V. Valet parking $14.

This tiny but friendly hotel with a marvelously helpful staff is in a great location right off Bourbon. Second floor rooms all have fresh striped wallpaper and antiques, but quality varies from big canopy beds to painted iron bedsteads. Bathrooms can be ultratiny.

✪ **Royal Street Inn & R Bar.** 1431 Royal St., New Orleans, LA 70116. ☎ **800/449-5535** or 504/948-7499. Fax 504/943-9880. www.royalstreetinn.com. 5 units. A/C TV TEL. $75 double; $100 suite. Rates include bar beverage.

This is a funky, happening little establishment in a residential neighborhood with plenty of street parking and regular police patrols. There couldn't be a better choice for laid-back travelers. They still bill themselves as a B&B, that's for Bed and Beverage—the lobby is the highly enjoyable R Bar. You check in with the bartender, and you get two complimentary cocktails at night. Regular rooms are small but cute, with doors that open directly to the street. Suites are the best value near the Quarter.

2 Mid City/Esplanade

EXPENSIVE

✪ **The House on Bayou Road.** 2275 Bayou Rd., New Orleans, LA 70119. ☎ **800/882-2968** or 504/945-0992. Fax 504/945-0993. www.houseonbayouroad.com. 8 units, 2 cottages. A/C MINIBAR TEL. $150–$295 double. Rates include full breakfast. AE, MC, V. Free parking.

If you want to stay in a rural plantation setting but still be near the French Quarter, try the House on Bayou Road. Just off Esplanade Avenue, this intimate Creole plantation home, built in the late 1700s for a colonial Spanish diplomat, has been restored by owner Cynthia Reeves. The individually decorated rooms have a light, airy quality. The grounds are beautifully manicured, and there's an outdoor pool, Jacuzzi, patio, and screened-in porch. The House on Bayou Road serves a plantation-style breakfast, and during the day and in the evening there's access to a minirefrigerator filled with beverages.

3   Central Business District

VERY EXPENSIVE

✪ **Fairmont Hotel.** At University Place, 123 Baronne St., New Orleans, LA 70122. ☎ **800/527-4727** or 504/529-7111. Fax 504/529-4764. www.fairmont.com. 700 units. A/C TV TEL. $229–$289 double. Extra person $25. AE, DC, DISC, MC, V. Valet parking $15.

New Orleanians still sometimes think of this as the Roosevelt, and today's Fairmont Hotel upholds its predecessor's tradition of elegance. The lobby is marbled and, and the guest rooms—all spacious, with high ceilings and such extras as an electric shoe buffer—were overhauled in 1996. Beds are luxuriously turned out, with the finest all-cotton sheets and down pillows. Bathrooms have scales, oversized towels, and custom-made fixtures. For the business traveler, the Fairmont offers in-room computer hookups and fax machines in the suites. The Fairmont is a "grand hotel" in the old manner, but it's in a less than desirable neighborhood, so be very careful at night.

Dining: On Sunday, there's a sumptuous brunch. Bailey's, a casual bistro, serves three meals daily, and for fine dining, there's the romantic Sazerac Bar and Grill.

Amenities: Rooftop health club, pool, tennis courts, 24-hour room service, twice-daily maid service, concierge, multilingual staff, tour desk, baby-sitting, activities desk, laundry service, beauty shop, business center, gift shop, newsstand, currency exchange.

✪ **Hotel Inter-Continental.** 444 St. Charles Ave., New Orleans, LA 70130. ☎ **800/327-0200** or 504/525-5566. Fax 504/523-7310. 482 units. A/C MINIBAR TV TEL. $235–$295 single; $305–$325 double; $500–$2,000 suite. AE, CB, DC, DISC, MC, V. Valet parking $17.

The red granite Hotel Inter-Continental rises from the heart of the Central Business District, within walking distance of the French Quarter and the Mississippi River attractions. It's a favorite of groups and conventions. You should consider it, too. Ongoing renovations should have all the rooms redecorated by fall 2000. These handsome rooms feel quite luxurious and are the best in the immediate area, though probably too stuffy for families.

Dining: The large marble lobby showcases a cocktail lounge, gourmet meals are served in the Veranda Restaurant, and Pete's Pub serves lunch daily.

Amenities: A health club and a basic pool, plus a barber shop and beauty salon, gift shop, business center, 24-hour room service, laundry and dry cleaning service, concierge, shoe shine service.

✪ **Windsor Court.** 300 Gravier St., New Orleans, LA 70130. ☎ **800/ 262-2662** or 504/523-6000. Fax 504/596-4749. www.windsorcourthotel.com. 319 units. A/C MINIBAR TV TEL. $275–$385 standard double; $365–$485 junior suite; $425–$675 full suite; $700–$1,150 2-bedroom suite. Children under 12 stay free in parents' room. AE, CB, DC, DISC, MC, V. Valet parking $18.

Condé Nast Traveller voted the Windsor Court the Best Hotel in North America. The unassuming, somewhat office-building exterior is camouflage for the quiet but posh delights found within. Two corridors downstairs are minigalleries that display original 17th-, 18th-, and 19th-century art, and there's a plush reading area with an international newspaper rack on the second floor. Everything is very, very chic. The level of service is extraordinarily high. The accommodations are exceptionally spacious, with classy, not flashy decor. All are suites, featuring large bay windows or a private balcony overlooking the river or the city, a private foyer, a large living room, a bedroom with French doors, a large marble bathroom with particularly luxe amenities, two dressing rooms, and a "petite kitchen."

Dining/Diversions: The Polo Club Lounge has the ambience of a private English club; the exceptional Grill Room Restaurant serves breakfast, brunch, lunch, and dinner. Le Salon, the lobby lounge, serves afternoon tea, cocktails, and sweets, and has chamber music and piano music during the day and evening.

Amenities: Health club with resort-size pool, sauna, and steam room; 24-hour suite service; concierge; laundry and dry cleaning; newspaper delivery; in-room massage.

EXPENSIVE

✪ **Hilton New Orleans Riverside Hotel.** 2 Poydras St., New Orleans, LA 70140. ☎ **800/445-8667** or 504/561-0500. Fax 504/568-1721. www.neworleans.hilton.com. 1,600 units. A/C MINIBAR TV TEL. $174–$314 double; $540–$2,000 suite. Special packages available. AE, CB, DC, DISC, JCB, MC, V. Valet parking $16; self-parking $12.

The Hilton is in the neighborhood of the Windsor Court, but in a more central location—right at the riverfront, near the World Trade Center of New Orleans, the New Orleans Convention Center, and the Aquarium. It's a self-contained complex of nearly a dozen restaurants, bistros, and bars; two gift shops; a full racquet and health club; a huge exhibition space; and no fewer than 38 conference rooms. In addition, Hilton's Flamingo Casino and the Riverwalk Marketplace are accessible from the hotel's lobby, which contains a nine-story atrium. Guest rooms are spacious, and most have fabulous views of the river or the city.

Dining/Diversions: The atrium is broken up into the English Bar, Le Café Bromeliad, and the French Garden Bar. Pete Fountain moved his jazz club from the Quarter to a third-floor replica here. The Flamingo is currently the only casino operating in the downtown area.

Amenities: 24-hour room service, concierge, laundry, dry cleaning, and pressing service, airport transportation, newspaper delivery, shoe-shine service. Guests are eligible for membership ($20 for 3 days) in the hotel's Rivercenter Racquet and Health Club.

Hyatt Regency. 500 Poydras Plaza, New Orleans, LA 70113. ☎ **800/ 233-1234** or 504/561-1234. Fax 504/587-4141. www.hyatt.com. 1,184 units. A/C TV TEL. $219–$244 double; $400–$625 suite. AE, DC, DISC, MC, V. Valet parking $15.

If your trip to New Orleans revolves around an event at the Superdome, you should consider the Hyatt. The hotel occupies a 32-story building, with guest rooms surrounding a seemingly bottomless central atrium. The public spaces are in grand corporate style, and so, as you'd expect, the lobby cafes generally attract a lunchtime crowd from the Central Business District. Guest rooms were clearly designed with the business traveler and the conventioneer in mind.

Dining/Diversions: The Courtyard serves regional fare at breakfast, lunch, and dinner. Top of the Dome Steakhouse is an upscale, revolving rooftop steak and seafood restaurant, open for dinner only. Hyttops Sports Bar & Grill serves pizza and burgers at lunch and dinner. The Mint Julep Lounge sometimes features live jazz.

Amenities: Heated rooftop pool, whirlpool, exercise room, free shuttle service to the French Quarter, concierge, room service, babysitting, currency exchange, business center, multilingual staff.

✪ **International House.** 221 Camp St., New Orleans, LA 70130. ☎ **800/ 633-5770** or 504/553-9550. Fax 504/200-6532. www.ihhotel.com. 119 units. A/C MINIBAR TV TEL. $180–$289 double; $359–$439 suite. Rates include continental breakfast. AE, MC, V. Valet parking.

Everyone's favorite new hotel, the International House, with creative design and meticulous attention to detail, has set a new standard. A wonderful old beaux arts bank building has been transformed into a modern space that still pays tribute to its locale. Consequently, in the graceful lobby, classical pilasters stand next to modern wrought iron chandeliers. Interiors are the embodiment of minimalist chic. Rooms are simple, with muted, monochromatic (okay, beige) tones, tall ceilings and ceiling fans, but also black-and-white photos of local musicians and characters, books about the city, and other clever decorating touches that anchor the room in its New Orleans setting.

Dining: Lemon Grass is a branch of a popular local restaurant. The bar is a hip hangout already, particularly at night as candles flicker and music plays.

Amenities: Room service, newspapers, fitness center, gift shop, dry cleaning, meeting rooms.

Wyndham Riverfront Hotel. 701 Convention Center Blvd., New Orleans, LA 70130. ☎ **800/WYNDHAM** or 504/524-8200. Fax 504/524-0600. www.wyndham.com. 202 units. A/C TV TEL. $175–$220 double. AE, CB, DC, DISC, MC, V. Valet parking $15.

There couldn't be a better location for the Convention Center: It's right across the street. But the rooms feel less business hotel and more, well, "use-convention-as-excuse-for-New Orleans-junket." Instead, rooms are prefab elegant, with stately wallpaper and armchairs, far more aesthetically pleasing than most big hotels. We did get a sense that the staff can be somewhat overwhelmed when a convention is staying there, but they were never less than gracious.

Dining: E's Restaurant serves Creole and continental fare at breakfast, lunch, and dinner. There's a lounge in the lobby.

Amenities: Room service until 11pm, laundry and dry cleaning, newspaper delivery, express checkout, concierge, exercise room, gift shop.

MODERATE

Holiday Inn Downtown–Superdome. 330 Loyola Ave., New Orleans, LA 70112. ☎ **800/535-7830** or 504/581-1600. Fax 504/522-0073. www.holidayinn.com/hotels/msydt. 297 units. A/C TV TEL. $94–$209 double; $350 suite. Extra person $15. Children under 20 stay free in parents' room. AE, CB, DC, DISC, JCB, MC, V. Parking $11.

The 18-story Holiday Inn Downtown–Superdome is centrally located, with easy access to the business and financial centers, the Louisiana Superdome (duh!), and the French Quarter. Each room has a balcony and city view, and the hotel has a collection of jazz scene murals available for public viewing. The dining room holds an interesting collection of New Orleans streetcar paintings. The Mardi Gras Lounge offers cocktails and after-dinner drinks nightly. There's a heated pool on the roof.

Le Pavillion Hotel. 833 Poydras St., New Orleans, LA 70140. ☎ **800/535-9095** or 504/581-3111. Fax 504/522-5543. www.lepavillion.com. 226 units. A/C MINIBAR TV TEL. $105–$370 double; $495–$1,495 suite. AE, CB, DC, DISC, MC, V. Valet parking $18.

Established in 1907 in a prime Central Business District location, Le Pavillion was the first hotel in New Orleans to have elevators; it's now a member of Historic Hotels of America. The lobby is stunning, with high ceilings, grand columns, plush furnishings, Oriental rugs, detailed woodwork, and 11 crystal chandeliers imported from Czechoslovakia. The standard guest rooms all have similar furnishings, but they differ in size. The hotel offers 24-hour room service, laundry and dry cleaning, newspaper delivery, baby-sitting, complimentary shoe shine, and a concierge. The large Gold Room dining room serves three meals daily and has a working fireplace. Complimentary hors d'oeuvres are served weekdays from 4 to 7pm in the Gallery lounge, and peanut-butter-and-jelly sandwiches and milk are served each evening in the lobby. There's a heated pool on the roof, plus a fitness center and whirlpool spa.

INEXPENSIVE

The Depot at Madame Julia's. 7048 O'Keef St., New Orleans, LA 70130. ☎ **504/529-2952.** Fax 504/529-1908. 14 units, all with shared bathroom. $55 single; $65 double. AE, personal checks (if rooms are paid in advance).

The Depot is an alternative to more commercial hotels in the CBD, and takes up part of a whole complex of buildings dating from the 1800s. Low prices and a guest house environment mean a number of good things—including rooms with character and a proprietor who loves to help guests with all the details of their stay—but it also means shared bathrooms, rooms on the small and cozy side, and a location that, while quiet on the weekends, can get noisy in the mornings as the working neighborhood gets going. A mere 7 blocks (safe in the daytime) from the Quarter, it's a quick walk or a short streetcar ride, which makes it an affordable alternative to the Quarter's much more expensive accommodations.

The Prytania Inn. 1415 Prytania St., New Orleans, LA 70130. ☎ **504/566-1515.** Fax 504/566-1518. 130 units, 8 without bathroom. A/C TEL. $49–$69 double. Extra person $10–$15. AE, DISC, MC, V. Limited free off-street parking available.

As you linger over breakfast at the Prytania, you'll notice the diversity of the guests: a fair number of young international budget travelers, couples enjoying a romantic weekend, a family in town to visit a university student. All seem equally at home. The Prytania manages to seem like a hotel, a hostel, a guest house, and a B&B all at the same time—and all while providing quaint, comfortable accommodations at rock-bottom rates.

4 Uptown/Garden District

VERY EXPENSIVE

✪ **Pontchartrain Hotel**. 2031 St. Charles Ave., New Orleans, LA 70140. ☎ **800/777-6193** or 504/524-0581. Fax 504/529-1165. 104 units. A/C TV TEL. $95–$380 double. Extra person $10, except special events $25. Seasonal packages and special promotional rates available. AE, CB, DC, DISC, MC, V. Parking $13.

This dignified hotel has long been a local landmark, and if other, newer hotels make it seem slightly worn at the edges (though upgrades are fixing that), it still feels like the most romantic and elegant hotel in the world. Its discreet ambience and pampering still make it a choice for celebrities and dignitaries. The regular rooms, which are larger than most, have all gotten facelifts, including cedar-lined closets, cushy towels, and pedestal washbasins.

Dining/Diversions: Café Pontchartrain has a solid reputation among locals. Stop for a drink in the Bayou Bar, which features live entertainment at night.

Amenities: 24-hour room service, complimentary shoe shine, complimentary newspaper, access to nearby spa with health club and outdoor pool.

EXPENSIVE

✪ **The Grand Victorian Bed & Breakfast**. 2727 St. Charles Ave, New Orleans, LA 70130. ☎ **504/895-1104**. Fax 504/896-8688. E-mail: Brabe2727@aol.com. 8 units. A/C TV TEL. $150–$350 double. Rates include breakfast. AE, DISC, MC, V. Limited free off-street parking.

Owner Bonnie Rabe confounded and delighted her new St. Charles neighbors when she took a crumbling Queen Anne–style Victorian mansion right on the corner of Washington (2 blocks from Lafayette cemetery and Commander's Palace with a streetcar stop right in front) and over the course of many arduous months, resurrected it into a showcase B&B. The stunning rooms are full of antiques (each has a breathtaking four-poster or wood canopy bed), with the slightly fussy details demanded by big Victorian rooms. A generous continental breakfast is served and friendly Bonnie is ready with suggestions on how to spend your time.

MODERATE

The Columns. 3811 St. Charles Ave., New Orleans, LA 70115. ☎ **800/445-9308** or 504/899-9308. 20 units. A/C TEL. $90–$175 double. Rates include continental breakfast. AE, MC, V. Parking available on street.

Built in 1883, the building is one of the greatest examples of a late 19th-century Louisiana residence. The grand, columned porch is a highly popular evening scene thanks to the bar inside. The immediate interior is utterly smashing; we challenge any other hotel to match this grand staircase and stained glass window combination. Unfortunately, the magnificence of the setting is hurt by the relentlessly casual attitude towards the public areas. Too bad. This could be a deeply romantic hotel, ponderously Victorian, and we mean that in a good way. But bar revenue reigns supreme. Consequently, the prices may not be justified, fabulous hangout or no. Low-end rooms are cozy, with quilts and old bedsteads. High-end rooms are indeed—it's the difference between the master's room and the servants quarters.

✪ **The McKendrick–Breaux House.** 1474 Magazine St., New Orleans, LA 70130. ☎ **888/570-1700** or 504/586-1700. Fax 504/522-7138. 7 units. www.mckendrick-breaux.com. A/C TV TEL. $95–$175 double. Rates include breakfast. AE, MC, V. Limited free off-street parking available.

Owner Eddie Breaux saved this 1865 building just as it was about to fall down and turned it into one of the city's best B&Bs. It's not just that the antique-filled rooms are spacious (some of the bathrooms are downright huge), quaint, and meticulously decorated, but not fussy. It's not just that the public areas are simple, elegant, and comfortable. It's Breaux himself. You would be hard-pressed to find a better host. The location is right in the middle of the convenient Lower Garden District, named the Most Trendy Neighborhood in America by *Utne Reader* magazine.

INEXPENSIVE

Park View Guest House. 7004 St. Charles Ave., New Orleans, LA 70118. ☎ **888/533-0746** or 504/861-7564. Fax 504/861-1225. www.parkviewguesthouse.com. 23 units, 17 with bathroom. A/C TEL. $85 double without bathroom, $109 double with bathroom. Rates include continental breakfast. Extra person $10. AE, DISC, MC, V. Parking available on street.

If a true getaway to you means a step back in time, then come to this quite-Uptown guest house, which feels at once like a truly old fashioned hotel (it was built in 1881) and a glamorous Belle Epoch mansion with all the trimmings. Antique-filled rooms are becoming plusher every minute. All rooms have high ceilings, while some have balconies overlooking Audubon Park, which is right across the street. The St. Charles streetcar stops right outside.

St. Charles Guesthouse. 1748 Prytania St., New Orleans, LA 70130. ☎ **504/523-6556.** Fax 504/522-6340. E-mail: dhilton111@aol.com. 35 units, 23 with private bathroom. $35–$85 double. Rates include continental breakfast. AE, MC, V. Parking available on street.

Very much worth checking out for those on a budget, the St. Charles Guesthouse—the first such accommodation in the Garden District and much-copied over the last 20 years—is not fancy, but it's one of the friendliest hotels in town. Rooms are plain and run from the low-end "backpacker" lodgings, which have no air-conditioning, to larger chambers with air-conditioning and private bathrooms—nice enough, but nothing special. That's okay; the place does have the required New Orleans atmosphere elements, including the banana tree–ringed courtyard. And there's a pool. It's only a short walk through the quiet and very pretty neighborhood to the St. Charles Avenue streetcar line.

St. Charles Inn. 3636 St. Charles Ave., New Orleans, LA 70115. ☎ **800/489-9908** or 504/899-8888. Fax 504/899-8892. 40 units. A/C TV TEL. $70 double. Rates include continental breakfast. AE, DC, DISC, MC, V. Free parking.

If you want to stay uptown and don't need or want the pampering of a fancy hotel or precious guest house, you are probably looking for the St. Charles Inn. It's on the St. Charles Avenue streetcar line, and is convenient to Tulane and Loyola universities and Audubon Park. Each room has two double beds or a king-size bed. Facilities include a lounge and a restaurant. Breakfast is served in your room, and the morning newspaper is complimentary.

5 At the Airport

Downtown New Orleans is only a 15-minute drive from the airport (in Kenner). But if you've got an early-morning flight and you're worried about traffic, you might consider either of these two hotels, both of which offer airport transfer.

There's the **Hilton New Orleans Airport,** 901 Airline Dr., Kenner, LA 70062 (☎ **800/445-8667** or 504/469-5000; www.neworleansairport.hilton.com), if you want to spend a night in Kenner in style. A less expensive alternative to the Hilton is the **Holiday Inn New Orleans–Airport,** 2929 Williams Blvd., Kenner, LA 70062 (☎ **800/465-4329** or 504/467-5611).

5

Dining

Within a short time during a trip to New Orleans, you will find yourself talking less about the sights and more about food—if not constantly about food. What you ate already, what you are going to be eating later, what you wish you had time to eat. We are going to take a stand and say to heck with New York and San Francisco: New Orleans has the best food in the United States. (There are natives who will gladly fight you if you say otherwise.). This is the city where the great chefs of the world come to eat—if they don't work here already. Many people love to do nothing more than wax nostalgic about great meals they have had here, describing entrees in practically pornographic detail. It is nearly impossible to have a bad meal in this town; at worst, it will be mediocre, and with proper guidance, you should even be able to avoid that.

1 Restaurants by Cuisine

Whether you've a hankering for cheap Cajun in the Quarter or an expensive eclectic place near the Esplanade, this list of restaurants by cuisine might help you narrow it down. You'll note that some places are listed in more than one, as many New Orleans restaurants defy rigid classification.

AMERICAN & NEW AMERICAN

Emeril's (Central Business District, *E*)

G&E Courtyard Grill (French Quarter, *M*)

The Grill Room (Central Business District, *E*)

Mike's on the Avenue (Uptown/Garden District, *E*)

Nola (French Quarter, *E*)

Pelican Club (French Quarter, *E*)

Peristyle (French Quarter, *E*)

Red Bike (Central Business District, *M*)

Rémoulade (French Quarter, *M*)

CAJUN

Bon Ton Café (Central Business District, *M*)

Bozo's (Metairie, *M*)

Key to abbreviations: *E* = Expensive, *M* = Moderate, *I* = Inexpensive.

Brigtsen's (Uptown/Garden District, *E*)

Ernst's Café (Central Business District, *I*)

K-Paul's Louisiana Kitchen (French Quarter, *E*)

Olde N'Awlins Cookery (French Quarter, *M*)

COFFEE SHOPS

Clover Grill (French Quarter, *I*)

COFFEE, TEA & SWEETS

Café du Monde (French Quarter, *I*)

Kaldi's Coffee House and Museum (French Quarter, *I*)

CONTINENTAL

The Veranda Restaurant (Central Business District, *M*)

CREOLE

Antoine's (French Quarter, *E*)

Arnaud's (French Quarter, *E*)

Bacco (French Quarter, *E*)

Bizou (Central Business District, *E*)

Brennan's (French Quarter, *E*)

Brigtsen's (Uptown/Garden District, *E*)

Broussard's (French Quarter, *E*)

Christian's (Mid City/ Esplanade, *M*)

Commander's Palace (Uptown/Garden District, *E*)

Court of Two Sisters (French Quarter, *E*)

Delmonico's (Central Business District, *E*)

Dooky Chase (Mid City/ Esplanade, *M*)

Emeril's (Central Business District, *E*)

Ernst's Café (Central Business District, *I*)

Felix's Restaurant & Oyster Bar (French Quarter, *I*)

Gumbo Shop (French Quarter, *M*)

Kelsey's (Uptown/Garden District, *M*)

Mother's (Central Business District, *I*)

Mr. B's Bistro & Bar (French Quarter, *M*)

Nola (French Quarter, *E*)

Olde N'Awlins Cookery (French Quarter, *M*)

Palace Café (Central Business District, *M*)

Praline Connection (French Quarter, *I*)

Ralph & Kacoo's (French Quarter, *M*)

Rémoulade (French Quarter, *M*)

Rita's Olde French Quarter Restaurant (French Quarter, *M*)

Tujague's (French Quarter, *M*)

Upperline (Uptown/ Garden District, *E*)

The Veranda Restaurant (Central Business District, *M*)

ECLECTIC

Bella Luna (French Quarter, *E*)

Red Bike (Central Business District, *M*)

Upperline (Uptown/ Garden District, *E*)

FRENCH

Brennan's (French Quarter, *E*)

Cafe Degas (Mid City/ Esplanade, *M*)

Crozier's Restaurant Français (Metairie, *M*)

Galatoire's (French Quarter, *E*)

Peristyle (French Quarter, *E*)

HAMBURGERS

Camellia Grill (Uptown/ Garden District, *I*)

INTERNATIONAL

Bayona (French Quarter, *E*)

Gabrielle (Mid City/ Esplanade, *M*)

Gautreau's (Uptown/ Garden District, *M*)

Mike's on the Avenue (Uptown/Garden District, *E*)

ITALIAN

Angeli On Decatur (French Quarter, *I*)

Bacco (French Quarter, *E*)

Bella Luna (French Quarter, *E*)

Figaro's Pizzeria (Uptown/ Garden District, *I*)

Pascal's Manale (Uptown/ Garden District, *M*)

Peristyle (French Quarter, *E*)

MEDITERRANEAN

Angeli On Decatur (French Quarter, *I*)

Mystic Cafe (Uptown/ Garden District, I)

PIZZA

Figaro's Pizzeria (Uptown/ Garden District, *I*)

SANDWICHES

Acme Oyster House (French Quarter, *I*)

Café Maspero (French Quarter, *I*)

Camellia Grill (Uptown/ Garden District, *I*)

Johnny's Po-Boys (French Quarter, *I*)

Mother's (Central Business District, *I*)

Uglesich's Restaurant & Bar (Central Business District, *I*)

SEAFOOD

Acme Oyster House (French Quarter, *I*)

Bozo's (Metairie, *M*)

Café Maspero (French Quarter, *I*)

Casamento's (Uptown/ Garden District, *I*)

Felix's Restaurant & Oyster Bar (French Quarter, *I*)

Olde N'Awlins Cookery
(French Quarter, *M*)
Pascal's Manale (Uptown/
Garden District, *M*)
Ralph & Kacoo's (French
Quarter, *M*)
Red Fish Grill (French
Quarter, *M*)
Uglesich's Restaurant &
Bar (Central Business
District, *I*)

SOUL FOOD

Dooky Chase (Mid City/
Esplanade, *M*)
Praline Connection (French
Quarter, *I*)

STEAK

Dickie Brennan's
Steakhouse (French
Quarter, *E*)
Pascal's Manale (Uptown/
Garden District, *M*)

VEGETARIAN

Old Dog New Trick
(French Quarter, *I*)

VIETNAMESE

Lemon Grass (Central
Business District, *M*)

2 The French Quarter

EXPENSIVE

Antoine's. 713 St. Louis St. ☎ **504/581-4422.** Reservations required. Main courses $14.25–$49. AE, CB, DC, MC, V. Mon–Sat 11:30am–2pm and 5:30–9:30pm. CREOLE.

Owned and operated by the same family for an astonishing 150 years, Antoine's is, unfortunately, beginning to show its age. With its 15 dining rooms and massive menu (more than 150 items), it was once the ultimate in fine dining in New Orleans. But murmurs about a decline in quality have become open complaints. Still, it's hard to ignore a legend, and so with some caution you may wish to investigate for yourself. Be sure to try the famous oysters Rockefeller (served hot in the shell, covered with a mysterious green sauce).

✪ **Arnaud's.** 813 Bienville St. ☎ **504/523-5433.** Reservations recommended. Jackets required in main dining room. Main courses $17–$28. AE, DC, MC, V, DISC. Mon–Fri 11:30am–2:30pm, Sun Jazz brunch 10am–2:30pm; Sun–Thurs 6–10pm, Fri–Sat 6–10:30pm. CREOLE.

It's hard to maintain a reputation throughout a century. So it is a great relief to report that the food at Arnaud's is still solidly good, and often excellent. The mosaic-tile floors, dark-wood paneling, ceiling medallions, and antique ceiling fans all make you feel as though you are dining in turn-of-the-century New Orleans. Rave-producing fish dishes included snapper or trout Pontchartrain (it's topped with crabmeat) and the spicy Pompano Duarte. Any filet mignon entree is superb. At lunch there's an inexpensive table d'hôte (fixed-price) selection along with an à la carte menu.

✪ **Bacco.** 310 Chartres St. ☎ **504/522-2426.** Reservations recommended. Main courses $19.50–$25. AE, CB, DC, MC, V. Daily 6–10pm; Sun brunch 10am–2pm. ITALIAN/CREOLE.

Don't expect spaghetti and marinara sauce here. Instead, think arresting, rich, ecstasy-inducing creations such as ravioli ripieni di formaggio, featuring four creamy cheeses all melting into a sauce of olive oil, tomatoes and browned garlic. Bacco is romantic and candlelit at night, more affordable and casual at lunchtime. Desserts are far above average, including possibly the best version of tiramisu we've ever had.

✪ **Bayona.** 430 Dauphine St. ☎ **504/525-4455.** Reservations required at dinner, recommended at lunch. Main courses $9–$12 at lunch, $14–$23 at dinner. AE, CB, DC, DISC, MC, V. Mon–Fri 11:30am–1:30pm; Mon–Thurs 6–9:30pm, Fri–Sat 6–10:30pm. INTERNATIONAL.

One of the city's top dining experiences, Bayona is beloved by savvy New Orleanians. Chef Susan Spicer, who honed her considerable skills in France, offers elegant, eclectic contemporary cuisine with Asian and Mediterranean flavors. The wine selection is extensive, and the staff is extremely helpful in suggesting the right wine. After a quiet, romantic evening at Bayona, you may well applaud next time you pass by.

✪ **Bella Luna.** 914 N. Peters St. ☎ **504/529-1583.** Reservations recommended. Main courses $16–$24.75. AE, DC, DISC, MC, V. Mon–Sat 6–10:30pm, Sun 6–9:30pm. ECLECTIC/ITALIAN/CONTINENTAL.

The expansive view of the Mississippi River—probably the best reason to go here—makes this perhaps the most romantic restaurant in New Orleans. Chef Horst Pfeifer, originally from Germany, eludes categories and draws upon almost every imaginable cuisine. Pastas are a specialty. Try the penne with peppers, eggplant, and Gorgonzola with a fontina sauce.

✪ **Brennan's.** 417 Royal St. ☎ **504/525-9711.** Reservations recommended. Main courses $18–$35 at lunch, $28.50–$38.50 at dinner. AE, CB, DC, DISC, MC, V. Daily 8am–2:30pm and 6–10pm. Closed Dec 25. FRENCH/HAUTE CREOLE.

For more than 40 years, breakfast at Brennan's has been a New Orleans tradition, a multi-course extravaganza that is unashamedly sauce- and egg-intensive. Dine here and you will find yourself rubbing elbows

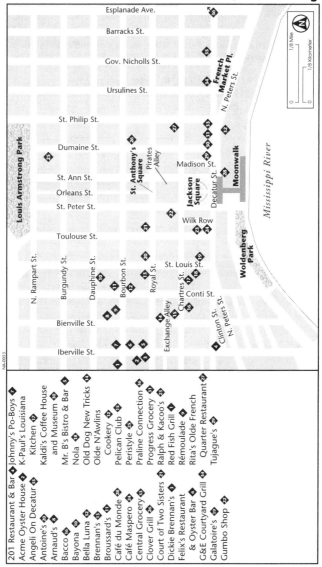

Esplanade Ave.

Barracks St.

Gov. Nicholls St.

Ursulines St.

St. Philip St.

Dumaine St.

St. Ann St.

Orleans St.

St. Peter St.

Toulouse St.

Louis Armstrong Park

N. Rampart St.

Burgundy St.

Dauphine St.

Bourbon St.

Royal St.

St. Anthony's Square

Pirates Alley

Madison St.

Jackson Square

Wilk Row

St. Louis St.

Chartres St.

Conti St.

Exchange Alley

Bienville St.

Iberville St.

Clinton St.

N. Peters St.

French Market Pl.

Decatur St.

Moonwalk

Woldenberg Park

Mississippi River

1/8 Mile
1/8 Kilometer

201 Restaurant & Bar
Acme Oyster House
Angeli On Decatur
Antoine's
Arnaud's
Bacco
Bayona
Bella Luna
Brennan's
Broussard's
Café du Monde
Café Maspero
Central Grocery
Clover Grill
Court of Two Sisters
Dickie Brennan's
Felix's Restaurant
 & Oyster Bar
G&E Courtyard Grill
Galatoire's
Gumbo Shop

Johnny's Po-Boys
K-Paul's Louisiana
 Kitchen
Kaldi's Coffee House
 and Museum
Mr. B's Bistro & Bar
Nola
Old Dog New Tricks
Olde N'Awlins
 Cookery
Pelican Club
Peristyle
Praline Connection
Progress Grocery
Ralph & Kacoo's
Red Fish Grill
Rémoulade
Rita's Olde French
 Quarter Restaurant
Tujague's

NA-0053

with loyal locals (including transplant Trent Reznor, Nine Inch Nails leader, who is a regular and a favorite of the staff) and tourists in search of a classic. Breakfast and lunch are quite crowded; dinner is less so (head straight to the gaslamp-lined balcony for dinner).

Broussard's. 819 Conti St. ☎ **504/581-3866.** Reservations recommended. No jeans, shorts, sneakers, or T-shirts. Main courses $19.50–$33. AE, MC, V. Daily 5:30–10pm. CREOLE.

After a period in which it relied more on its landmark status than on its food to attract patrons, Broussard's is back. Along with fine French-Creole standbys like oysters Broussard's (with crabmeat and a cream sauce with Brie and artichokes), you'll find many innovative creations. The house dessert specialty is "Delice Madam P," a plate of three desserts, such as puff pastry, cheesecake with praline sauce, and strawberries with custard sauce.

Court of Two Sisters. 613 Royal St. ☎ **504/522-7261.** Reservations required at dinner. Main courses $15.50–$30; fixed-price menu $37; brunch $21. AE, CB, DC, DISC, MC, V. Daily 9am–3pm and 5:30–10pm. CREOLE.

The ambience here is more of draw than the food, but what a draw it is. You enter through a huge courtyard filled with flowers, fountains, and low-hanging willows, with a wishing well at its center. You can dine outside amid the greenery or in the Royal Court Room. The daily jazz brunch buffet features more than 60 dishes (meat, fowl, fish, vegetables, fresh fruits, homemade bread, and pastries) and a strolling jazz band. Delicacies such as shrimp Toulouse, crawfish Louise, and chicken Michelle are good bets at dinner.

Dickie Brennan's Steakhouse. 716 Iberville St. ☎ **504/522-2467.** Reservations suggested. Main courses $14.95–$32. AE, DC, DISC, MC, V. Mon–Fri 11:30am–2:30pm, 5:30–10pm. Sat–Sun 5:30–11pm. STEAK.

Carnivores should be pleased with this latest Brennan family establishment, which has the feel of a contemporary clubhouse. It's a little busy, but you'll enjoy it. All the meat is USDA Prime and great care is taken to cook it just as the customer dictates. The House Filet comes surrounded by quite good creamy spinach and Pontalba potatoes. Don't miss their Bananas Foster Bread Pudding, which proves there can still be new twists on this old faithful dish.

✪ **Galatoire's.** 209 Bourbon St. ☎ **504/525-2021.** Reservations accepted Tues–Thurs only, and only for parties of 8 or more. Jackets required after 5pm and all day Sun. Main courses $14–$22. AE, MC, V, DC. Sun noon–9pm, Tues–Sat 11:30am–9pm. Closed holidays. FRENCH.

The venerated Galatoire's causes heated discussions these days among local foodies: still the best restaurant in New Orleans, or past its prime? Locals love it because they've gone for regular Sunday evening dinners for years, and all the old waiters know their names. We love it because in *A Streetcar Named Desire,* Stella took Blanche there to escape Stanley's poker game. It was Tennessee Williams' favorite restaurant (his table is the one right behind the word *Restaurant* on the window). Galatoire's is worth the trip, though you may not have the same experience as a knowledgeable local, unless you get a waiter who can really guide you (ask for John). For an entree, get the red snapper or redfish topped with sautéed crabmeat meunière—it will probably be one of the finest fish dishes you have during your stay.

K-Paul's Louisiana Kitchen. 416 Chartres St. ☎ **504/524-7394.** Reservations recommended for upstairs dining room. Main courses $6.95–$14 at lunch, $20.95–$30 at dinner. AE, CB, DC, MC, V. Mon–Sat 11:30am–2:30pm and 5:30–10:30pm. CAJUN.

Paul Prudhomme was at the center of the Cajun revolution of the early '80s, when Cajun food became known throughout the world. His reputation and his line of spices continue today, which is probably why there is constantly a line outside his restaurant. Unfortunately, while the food is still good, it's not spectacular and certainly is not worth the wait (upwards of $1^1/_2$ hours). The portions are Paul-sized, and as spicy as you might imagine, but nothing that special. It feels as if the menu hasn't changed all that dramatically in quite some time.

Nola. 534 St. Louis St. ☎ **504/522-6652.** Reservations recommended. Main courses $16–$30. AE, DC, DISC, MC, V. Mon–Sat 11:30am–2pm; Mon–Thurs 6–10pm, Fri–Sat 6pm–midnight, Sun 6–10pm. CREOLE/NEW AMERICAN.

This is the more casual and less expensive of chef Emeril Lagasse's two restaurants. The same problems that plague Emeril's, however, also surface here: fine food, but often-horrible attitude, and the potential for painfully slow service. Still, it's conveniently located in the Quarter. And then there's the food: an appetizer that's a sort of deconstructed roast beef sandwich, unique entrees like Caribbean-style grilled free-range chicken and cedar-plank fish.

✪ **Pelican Club.** 312 Exchange Alley. ☎ **504/523-1504.** Reservations recommended. Main courses $18.50–$24; fixed-price early dinner $17.95. AE, DC, DISC, MC, V. Mon–Thurs 5pm–closing, Fri–Sun 5:30pm–closing. Early dinner Mon–Thurs 5–5:45pm. NEW AMERICAN.

Just a short stroll from the House of Blues, the Pelican Club is worth investigating, particularly for its reasonably priced three-course fixed-price meal. The appetizers are perhaps a bit more inventive than the entrees, but everything is quite tasty. The desserts are certainly standouts. Try the flat (rather than puffy) white chocolate bread pudding, creamy chocolate pecan pie, or amazing profiteroles. The mostly young wait staff is sassy in a good way, helpful and full of answers and opinions about the menu. Take advantage of them.

✪ **Peristyle.** 1041 Dumaine St. ☎ **504/593-9535.** Reservations recommended. Main courses $20–$24. AE, DC, MC, V. Fri 11:30am–2pm; Tues–Thurs 6–9pm, Fri–Sat 6–10:30pm. FRENCH/AMERICAN/ITALIAN BISTRO.

Chef Anne Kearney has done a beautiful job with Peristyle, which she purchased after the death of founding chef John Neal. In this dark, romantic bistro, she continues the restaurant's fine tradition of delicious, elegant meals and attentive service. The menu changes seasonally, and there are so many interesting choices that you'll want to go back to try many of them.

MODERATE

✪ **G&E Courtyard Grill.** 1113 Decatur St. ☎ **504/528-9376.** Reservations recommended. Main courses $12.50–$26. AE, CB, DC, DISC, MC, V. Fri–Sun 11:30am–2:30pm; Sun–Thurs 6–10pm, Fri–Sat 6–11pm. NEW AMERICAN.

The G&E has been open for nearly 10 years, but is still treated like a splashy new arrival, with a line frequently snaking out the door. Atmosphere junkies really like the covered courtyard, where cast-iron chairs and glass-topped tables rest on terra-cotta tile. The best part? The open grill at the back of the courtyard, where a dozen chickens can typically be seen spinning on the rotisserie. Another good choice is the grilled Gulf fish with chanterelle–black lentil sauce served with a risotto cake.

Gumbo Shop. 630 St. Peter St. ☎ **504/525-1486.** Main courses $5.95–$14.95. AE, CB, DC, DISC, JCB, MC, V. Daily 11am–11pm. CREOLE.

This is the cheap and convenient way to get solid, if not particularly memorable, classic Creole food. The Gumbo Shop is 1 block off Jackson Square in a building dating from 1795. It's a bit touristy, but not unappealing. The menu reads like a textbook list of traditional local food: red beans and rice, shrimp Creole, crawfish étouffée.

✪ **Mr. B's Bistro & Bar.** 201 Royal St. ☎ **504/523-2078.** Reservations recommended. Main courses $15.50–$28. AE, DC, DISC, MC, V. Mon–Sat 11:30am–3pm; Sun brunch 10:30am–2:30pm; daily 5:30–10pm. CONTEMPORARY CREOLE.

Run by Cindy Brennan, this deceptively simple place only helps so-lidify the Brennan reputation. The food, mostly modern interpretations of Creole classics, is simple, but with spices that elevate the flavors into something your mouth really thanks you for. The crab cakes are about as good as that dish gets. Superb too is the not-too-spicy andouille sausage.

Olde N'Awlins Cookery. 729 Conti St. ☎ **504/529-3663.** Reservations accepted for groups of 5 or more. Breakfast items $6–$11; complete breakfast $6; main courses $5.75–$14.75 at lunch, $14.50–$20.75 at dinner. AE, MC, V. Daily 7am–11pm. CREOLE/CAJUN/SEAFOOD.

A decent standby if your first choices are full, this family-operated restaurant serves up reliably good traditional Cajun and Creole favorites such as jambalaya, blackened redfish, and shrimp Creole. Housed in an 1849 building that's been a private house, a brothel, a bistro bar, and a disco, it makes use of the original old brick and a charming courtyard to create a very pleasant and—dare we say it?—decidedly New Orleans atmosphere. The restaurant also offers an extensive breakfast menu.

Ralph & Kacoo's. 519 Toulouse St. ☎ **504/522-5226.** Reservations recommended. Main courses $6.95–$17.95. AE, DC, DISC, MC, V. Mon–Thurs 11am–10pm, Fri–Sat 11am–11pm, Sun 11am–9:30pm. CREOLE/SEAFOOD.

This is a satisfying, reliable place for seafood, which is probably why it is usually crowded at all hours. The Creole dishes are quite good, portions are more than ample, prices are reasonable, and the high volume of business means everything is fresh. Be sure to try the satin pie for dessert.

Red Fish Grill. 115 Bourbon St. ☎ **504/598-1200.** Reservations limited. Main courses, lunch only $8.75–$9.75, dinner $8.95–$17.75. AE, MC, V. Mon–Sat 11am–3pm, Mon–Sun 5–11pm, Sun brunch 10am–3pm. SEAFOOD.

Red Fish is far better than anything else in its price range on Bourbon Street. Ralph Brennan's place—surprise, another Brennan restaurant—serves many New Orleans specialties, with an emphasis on—surprise again—fish. The signature dish is a pan-seared catfish topped with sweet potato crust and an andouille cream drizzle.

Rémoulade. 309 Bourbon St. ☎ **504/523-0377.** Reservations recommended. Main courses $4–$20. AE, CB, DC, MC, V, DISC. Daily 11:30am–midnight. CREOLE/AMERICAN.

If you've been wanting to go to Arnaud's but can't afford it, can't get a reservation, or just don't feel like dressing up, we have the answer: Rémoulade, a brasserie-like offshoot of the terribly formal Arnaud's, right next door. The menu is fun and eclectic, and the food, not surprisingly, is excellent. Thin-crust pizzas with a wide variety of toppings are popular, as are the seafood po' boys. Rémoulade also features some of the dishes Arnaud's made famous, like shrimp Arnaud (in a Creole mustard sauce) and oysters stewed in cream. The wine list comes from Arnaud's, so you won't be disappointed on that front, either.

Rita's Olde French Quarter Restaurant. 945 Chartres St. (at St. Philip St.). ☎ **504/525-7543.** Main courses $5.95–$11.95 at lunch, $13.95–$17.95 at dinner. AE, CB, DC, DISC, MC, V. Daily 11am–10pm. CREOLE.

Rita's doesn't look like much on the outside, and you're likely to walk right past without noticing it. Don't. When you walk in, you'll feel right at home. The atmosphere is very casual, the staff friendly and inviting. The menu is extensive, featuring at least 20 entrees, including pasta and veal dishes. The oyster and artichoke soup is tasty, and the gumbo is excellent. You shouldn't miss Rita's bread pudding, and you probably won't—they often bring out a complimentary dish when you're done with your meal.

201 Restaurant & Bar. 201 Decatur St. (at Iberville). ☎ **504/561-0007.** Reservations recommended. Main courses $15–$18. AE, DC, DISC, MC, V. Mon–Fri 11am–3pm; Sun–Thurs 5–11pm, Fri–Sat 5pm–midnight. CONTEMPORARY LOUISIANA.

They do fish very nicely, with a decided Asian influence, at this casual but spiffy place. It's won praise as one of the 10 best new restaurants of the year (given the number of restaurants in town, it's tough competition). It's a simple space, a typical New Orleans high-ceilinged room, mercifully largely untampered with except for the addition of some modern and Depression-era lamps.

Tujague's. 823 Decatur St. ☎ **504/525-8676.** Reservations recommended. 4-course lunch $6.50–$13.95; 6-course dinner $24.95–$29.95. AE, CB, DC, DISC, MC, V. Daily 11am–3pm and 5–10:30pm. CREOLE.

Tujague's (pronounced *two-jacks*) is the second restaurant to occupy this site. The first was run by Madame Begue, who in 1856 began cooking huge and well-loved "second breakfasts" for the butchers who worked in the French Market across the way. Today, Tujague's serves only lunch and dinner, but continues the Begue's tradition of serving whatever inspiration dictates. This place is a favorite with New Orleanians, who don't seem to mind the very limited menu.

INEXPENSIVE

Acme Oyster House. 724 Iberville St. ☎ **504/522-5973.** Reservations not accepted. Oysters $3.50–$6; po' boys $4.75–$6.95; New Orleans specialties

$5.50–$6.95; seafood $9.95–$12.95. AE, DC, DISC, JCB, MC, V. Mon–Sat 11am–10pm, Sun noon–7pm. SEAFOOD/SANDWICHES.

This joint is always loud, often crowded, and the kind of place where you're likely to run into obnoxious fellow travelers. But if you need an oyster fix, or if you've never tried oyster shooting (taking a raw oyster, possibly doused in sauce, and letting it slide right down your throat), come here. If you can't quite stomach them raw, try the oyster po' boy, with beer, of course.

✪ **Angeli On Decatur.** 1141 Decatur (at Gov. Nichols). ☎ **504/566-0077.** Everything under $10. AE, MC, V. 24 hours. ITALIAN/MEDITERRANEAN.

This is a brand-new, highly welcome addition to the Quarter, featuring terrific food. This place has already gotten raves for round-the-clock hours and local delivery service—all things hungry locals and tourists crave. It's perfect for a light, actually rather healthy meal, a needed alternative to some of the extravaganzas offered by more formal restaurants in town.

Café Maspero. 601 Decatur St. ☎ **504/523-6250.** Reservations not accepted. Main courses $4.25–$9. No credit cards. Sun–Thurs 11am–11pm, Fri–Sat 11am–midnight. SEAFOOD/SANDWICHES.

Upon hearing complaints about the increasing presence in the Quarter of "foreign" restaurants such as Subway and the Hard Rock Cafe, one local commented, "Good. That must mean the line will be shorter at Cafe Maspero." It serves burgers, deli sandwiches, seafood, grilled marinated chicken, and so on, in some of the largest portions you'll ever run into. And there's an impressive list of wines, beers, and cocktails, all delicious and all at low, low prices.

✪ **Clover Grill.** 900 Bourbon St. ☎ **504/598-1010.** All items under $7. AE, MC, V. Daily 24 hours. COFFEE SHOP.

The "Happiest Grill On Earth!" boasts the irreverent menu, which also claims "We're here to serve people and make them feel prettier than they are." The staff at this delightful 24-hour diner competes with the menu for fun. Juicy, perfect burgers are cooked under a hubcap; they say it seals in the juices, and it seems to work. So well, in fact, that we are going to break with tradition and declare them the best burgers in New Orleans. Breakfast is served around the clock.

Felix's Restaurant & Oyster Bar. 739 Iberville St. ☎ **504/522-4440.** Main courses $10–$19.75. AE, MC, V. Mon–Thurs 10am–midnight, Fri 10am–1am, Sat 10am–1:30am, Sun 10am–10pm. SEAFOOD/CREOLE.

Like its neighbor the Acme Oyster House, Felix's is a crowded and noisy place, full of locals and tourists taking advantage of the late

---

Whole Lotta Muffaletta Goin' On

Muffalettas are almost mythological sandwiches, enormous concoctions of round Italian bread, Italian cold cuts and cheeses, and olive salad. One person cannot eat a whole one—at least not in one sitting. (And if you can, don't complain to us about your stomachache.) Instead, share; a half makes a good meal and a quarter is a filling snack. They may not sound like much on paper, but once you try one, you'll be hooked.

Judging from the line that forms at lunchtime, many others agree with us that ✪ **Central Grocery,** 923 Decatur St. (☎ **504/523-1620**), makes the best muffaletta there is. A small but critical minority favors the muffalettas at **Progress Grocery,** 915 Decatur. between Dumaine and St. Philip (☎ **504/525-6627**). Take your sandwich across the street and eat it on the banks of the Mississippi for an inexpensive romantic meal (about $7 for a whole sandwich).

---

hours. Have your oysters raw, in a stew, in a soup, Rockefeller or Bienville style, in spaghetti, or even in an omelette. If oysters aren't your bag, the fried or grilled fish, chicken, steaks, spaghetti, omelets, and Creole cooking are mighty good, too.

Johnny's Po-Boys. 511 St. Louis St. ☎ **504/524-8129.** Everything under $8. Cash only. Mon–Fri 8am–4:30pm, Sat–Sun 9am–4pm. SANDWICHES.

For location, right near a busy part of the Quarter, and menu simplicity, po' boys and more po' boys, you can't ask for much more than Johnny's. They put anything you could possibly imagine (and some you couldn't) on huge hunks of French bread. Johnny boasts "even my failures are edible" and that says it all. And they deliver!

Old Dog New Trick. 307 Exchange Alley. ☎ **504/522-4569.** Main courses $6.95–$9.95. AE, MC, V. Daily 11:30am–9pm. VEGETARIAN.

You'd think this tiny cafe tucked away on equally tiny Exchange Alley would be lost, but judging from the crowds, local and tourist vegetarians have managed to find it. Large portions and small prices make this a pleasing, healthy stop. The cafe calls itself "vegan friendly." It does have dishes with cheese, but can make them without, and some tuna does sneak onto the menu. The sandwiches, salads, and stuffed pitas, not to mention polenta and a variety of tofu dishes, have been voted best vegetarian by *Gambit* readers. Delivery is available.

Praline Connection. 542 Frenchmen St., just outside the Quarter. ☎ **504/943-3934.** Reservations not accepted. Main courses $4–$13.95. AE, DC, DISC, MC, V. Sun–Thurs 11am–10:30pm, Fri–Sat 11am–midnight. CREOLE/SOUL FOOD.

Somewhat hidden away on Frenchmen Street is a popular but perhaps overrated restaurant with little ambience. Don't go for a romantic dinner, because the noise level can be daunting and the crowds so dense you might have to share a table. Praline Connection serves solid but undistinguished Creole and soul food, which some rave about but others find rather ordinary. Praline Connection II, 901 South Peters St. (☎ **504/523-3973**), offers the same menu and a larger dining room.

3 Mid City/Esplanade

MODERATE

Cafe Degas. 3127 Esplanade Ave. ☎ **504/945-5635.** Reservations recommended. Main courses $6.25–$18.50. AE, DC, DISC, MC, V. Mon–Fri 11:30am–2:30pm; Sat 10:30am–2:30pm brunch; Sun 10:30am–3:30pm brunch; Mon–Thurs 5:30pm–10pm, Fri–Sat 6–11pm. FRENCH.

A charming French bistro, warm and friendly with upscale rustic decor. The hearty food is rustic as well, with big but simple flavors in large portions of tasty, rich food. Desserts are delicious and homemade—the key lime tart is spectacular.

Christian's. 3835 Iberville St. ☎ **504/482-4924.** Reservations recommended. Main courses $15–$25. AE, DC, MC, V. Tues–Fri 11:30am–2pm; Tues–Sat 5:30–9:30pm. CREOLE.

Ever had a three-course meal in a church? Here's your chance. Renovations preserved the architecture, including the high-beamed ceiling and (secular) stained-glass windows. The old altar is the waiters' station, and the sermon board out front lists the menu. This is one of the city's great French-Creole restaurants, with locals accounting for about 80% of its clientele. The roasted duck is heavenly, as is the gumbo. Daily fish specials are delightful.

✪ **Dooky Chase.** 2301 Orleans Ave. ☎ **504/821-0600** or 504/821-2294. Reservations recommended at dinner. Main courses $10–$17.50; fixed-price 4-course meal $25; Creole feast $37.50. AE, DC, MC, V. Sun–Thurs 11:30am–10pm, Fri–Sat 11:30am–11pm. SOUL FOOD/CREOLE.

African and African American influences are key components in New Orleans' multicultural cuisine. In the elegant dining rooms of Dooky Chase, classic soul food interacts gloriously with the city's French, Sicilian, and Italian traditions. Chef Leah Chase dishes up one of New

Orleans' best bowls of gumbo—no small achievement—along with more esoteric dishes such as shrimp Clemenceau, an unlikely but successful casserole of sautéed shellfish, mushrooms, peas, and potatoes. The fried chicken is exquisite. Prices are a bit high and service less than brisk—though always friendly—but Dooky Chase offers very good food and a vintage New Orleans experience. Take a cab.

✪ **Gabrielle.** 3201 Esplanade Ave. ☎ **504/948-6233.** Reservations recommended. Main courses $16–$28; early evening special (Tues–Thurs 5:30–6:15pm) $16.98. AE, CB, DC, DISC, MC, V. Oct–May Fri 11:30am–2pm; year-round Tues–Sat 5:30–10pm. INTERNATIONAL.

This rather small, but casually elegant restaurant on Esplanade Avenue, just outside the French Quarter, is gaining a big reputation around town thanks to some superb food from a chef who studied under Paul Prudhomme and Frank Brigtsen. A foie gras with fig sauce appetizer features a generous portion that melts in your mouth. For a main course, you can't go wrong with any fish on the menu, from the pompano cooked in paper with garlic and tomatoes to the panfried trout with shrimp and roasted pecan butter. A standout was the double-thick-cut pork chop with a tomato salsa, topped with stuffed Anaheim chili—it had some masterful flavors. Gabrielle offers an early evening special Tuesday through Thursday from 5:30 to 6:15pm. You'll get a choice of three appetizers, two entrees, and two desserts for only $15.95.

4 Central Business District

EXPENSIVE

Bizou. 701 St. Charles Ave. ☎ **504/524-4114.** Reservations recommended. Main courses $9.50–$22. AE, DC, MC, V. Mon–Fri 11am–3pm; Tues–Sat 5–10pm. CREOLE.

Bizou (French for "little kiss") is making a strong move to become the best little bistro in the Central Business District. A very strong, innovative menu includes very good rabbit chasseur (with mushrooms, tomatoes, and crawfish) and filet mignon (stuffed with oyster dressing, accompanied by garlic mashed potatoes and portobello mushrooms), but the salmon medallions with fried spinach sets an even higher standard.

Delmonico's. 1300 St. Charles Ave. ☎ **504/525-4937.** Reservations required. Main course $18–$30. AE, DC, DISC, MC, V. Lunch Mon–Fri 11:30am–2pm, dinner Sun–Thurs 6–10pm, Fri–Sat 6–11pm, brunch Sun 10:30am–2pm. CREOLE.

This is the latest venture by the ubiquitous and spirited Emeril Lagasse. Delmonico's is less a chance for him to show off the innovative cooking that has made him a star, and more a chance to experiment with classic Creole dishes. Emeril renovated the building, and the result is one of the loveliest interiors in New Orleans, simultaneously evoking its glorious past (though surely it never looked this good), but with fresh, modern touches. If you don't like rich, sauce-intensive food, this menu won't appeal to you. But it's fun to see what Emeril is up to in this context.

✪ **Emeril's.** 800 Tchoupitoulas St. ☎ **504/528-9393.** Reservations required at dinner. Main courses $18–$32; menu degustation $75. AE, CB, DC, DISC, MC, V. Mon–Fri 11:30am–2pm; Mon–Thurs 6–10pm, Fri–Sat 6–11pm. CREOLE/ NEW AMERICAN.

Ecstasy. Emeril Lagasse isn't just the boisterous and charismatic chef who has gained nationwide popularity from his programs on cable's TV Food Network. He is one of the Crescent City's finest chefs, and one of America's finest as well. There are arguments about the service. Some diners find it snooty and sometimes downright rude. What is never in question is the quality of the food. Emeril's specialty is what he calls *New* New Orleans Cuisine, based upon and using key ingredients of Creole classics but taking them in new and exciting directions. Portions are gargantuan, each plate dances with color and texture, and side dishes are perfectly paired with entrees. The signature dessert, astonishingly rich banana cream pie with banana crust and caramel drizzle sauce, will leave you moaning and pounding on the table (we've seen it happen).

✪ **The Grill Room.** In the Windsor Court Hotel, 300 Gravier St. ☎ **504/ 522-1992.** Jacket and tie required. Reservations recommended. Main courses $11–$19.50 at lunch, $28–$39 at dinner. AE, CB, DC, DISC, MC, V. Mon–Thurs 7–10:30am, Fri–Sat 7:30–10:30pm, Sun 7–9am; Mon–Sat 11:30am–2pm, Sun brunch 9am–2pm; Sun–Thurs 6–10pm, Fri–Sat 6–10:30pm. NEW AMERICAN.

This is a special-event place, where the silverware is heavy, the linens thick, and all diners dressed to the nines. The Grill Room is an elegant and stately place whose chefs constantly win culinary awards and whose cuisine, service, and wine list are all flawless. The restaurant has an upper-crust-English-meets-upper-crust-Southern character, evident in everything from its 19th-century British paintings and selection of teas to the gracious, attentive service. So sit back and enjoy what should be an exceptional meal.

MODERATE

Bon Ton Café. 401 Magazine St. ☎ **504/524-3386.** Reservations required at dinner. Main courses $8.75–$19.75 at lunch, $19.75–$25.25 at dinner. AE, DC, MC, V. Mon–Fri 11am–2pm and 5–9:30pm. CAJUN.

New Orleans Dining

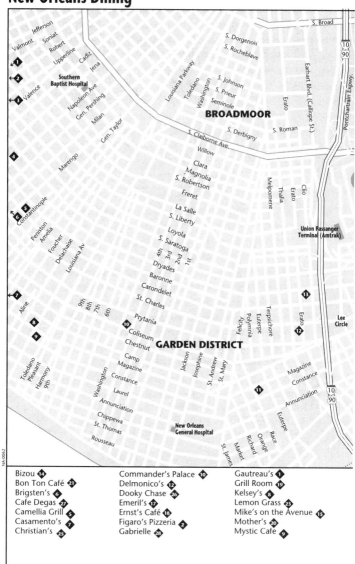

Bizou ⓮
Bon Ton Café ㉑
Brigsten's ❻
Cafe Degas ㉗
Camellia Grill ❺
Casamento's ❼
Christian's ㉔

Commander's Palace ⓰
Delmonico's ⓲
Dooky Chase ㉖
Emeril's ⓱
Ernst's Café ⓯
Figaro's Pizzeria ❷
Gabrielle ㉘

Gautreau's ❶
Grill Room ⓳
Kelsey's ❽
Lemon Grass ㉓
Mike's on the Avenue ⓭
Mother's ⓴
Mystic Cafe ❾

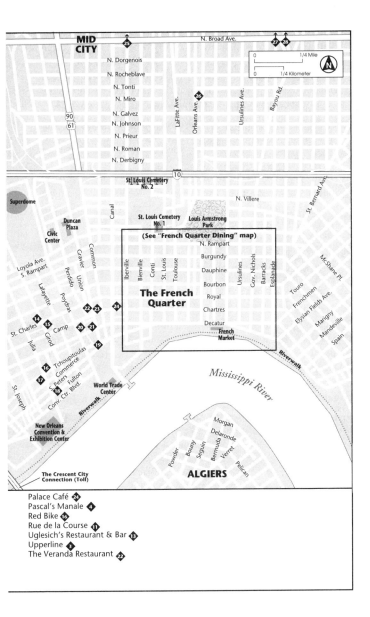

Palace Café 24
Pascal's Manale 4
Red Bike 16
Rue de la Course 11
Uglesich's Restaurant & Bar 13
Upperline 3
The Veranda Restaurant 22

75

Al and Wayne grew up in bayou country, where Al learned Cajun cooking from his mother. He came to New Orleans in 1936, bought the Bon Ton in 1953, and since then has been serving up seafood gumbo, crawfish bisque, jambalaya, crawfish omelettes, and other Cajun dishes in a manner that would make his mother proud.

Lemon Grass. 221 Camp St. (in the International House). ☎ **504/553-9550.** Reservations suggested. Main courses $12.95–$18.95. AE, MC, V. Daily breakfast 7:30–9am, lunch 11:30am–2:30pm, dinner Mon–Thurs 6–10pm, Fri–Sun 6–11pm. VIETNAMESE.

Lemon Grass' Chef Minh went directly from waiting tables at Emeril's to opening up his own restaurant—a bold move in a town so fiercely competitive for dining patrons. But in less than 4 years, his modern Vietnamese cuisine has become a favorite among local foodies.

✪ **Palace Café.** 605 Canal St. ☎ **504/523-1661.** Reservations recommended. Main courses $10.95–$24.95. AE, DC, DISC, MC, V. Mon–Fri 11:30am–2:30pm, Sat–Sun 7am–3pm (brunch 10:30am–2:30pm); daily 5:30–10pm. CONTEMPORARY CREOLE.

The Palace Café offers contemporary Creole food, with a strong emphasis on seafood. There are meat dishes on the menu, but *definitely* go for the seafood: catfish pecan meunière or andouille-crusted fish of the day, served with sides like ragout of crawfish tails, corn, peppers, and onions. Meanwhile, have fun observing the high-energy action in the open kitchen. Don't miss the near-ecstasy-inducing white chocolate bread pudding, a Palace Café original.

Red Bike. 746 Tchoupitoulas St. ☎ **504/529-BIKE.** Main courses $7–$11 at lunch, $9–$15 at dinner. AE, MC, V. Mon–Fri 11am–3pm, Sat–Sun Brunch 10am–3pm; Tues–Thurs 6–9:30pm; Sat–Sun 6–10pm. NEW AMERICAN/ECLECTIC.

Freshly under new management, the Red Bike is a fine choice if you are looking for a healthy alternative to the endless array of sauces offered elsewhere in the city. It's conveniently located in the warehouse district, making it a handy place for a pit stop during gallery hopping. Inside the attractive cafe setting, you will find all sorts of yummy sandwiches, on the house bread (which is for sale, along with other bakery delights, at the counter), including a recommended curried turkey salad. Salads are hearty and most menu selections use interesting cheeses, herbs, and veggies. Brunch can be particularly nice, with a variety of egg dishes. The prices here are so reasonable, the place teeters just on the edge of the "inexpensive" category.

The Veranda Restaurant. In the Hotel Inter-Continental, 444 St. Charles Ave. ☎ **504/585-4383.** Reservations recommended. Main courses $11.50–$22.50. AE, CB, DC, DISC, MC, V. Mon–Sun 6:30am–2pm and 5:30–10pm; Sun brunch 11am–2:30pm. CONTINENTAL/CREOLE.

Thanks to the glass-enclosed garden courtyard and private dining room, the Veranda feels like a stately New Orleans home, and Tuesday through Sunday a harpist makes dining all the more memorable.

The Veranda's chef, Willy Coln, is one of the most respected in New Orleans. The menu is varied, and it's doubtful you'll find anything to complain about. You might start with excellent Louisiana crab cakes in a light Creole mustard sauce. The oyster and artichoke soup is always good, and smoked duck and wild mushroom strudel is also a top choice. Entrees include potato-crusted redfish with baby bok choy and ginger beurre blanc. The breaded and panfried rabbit with Creole mustard sauce and the heart-healthy vegetable strudel on tomato coulis and fresh artichoke ragout are done to perfection. All the desserts are incredible.

INEXPENSIVE

Ernst's Café. 600 S. Peters St. ☎ **504/525-8544.** Main courses $6.50–$9.95. AE, DC, MC, V. Mon–Fri 11am–3pm. CAJUN/CREOLE.

The same family has run the restaurant and bar in this old brick building since 1902. Its brick walls, high ceilings, and heavy-timbered bar make it an interesting and attractive setting for excellent sandwiches, hamburgers, fried shrimp, salads, red beans and rice, and po' boys. If the weather is fine, eat outside.

✪ **Mother's.** 401 Poydras St. ☎ **504/523-9656.** Reservations not accepted. Menu items $1.75–$16.50. No credit cards. Mon–Sat 5am–10pm, Sun 7am–10pm. SANDWICHES/CREOLE.

Perhaps the proudest of all restaurants when New Orleans was named Fattest City in the U.S. was Mother's, whose overstuffed, mountain-sized po' boys absolutely helped contribute to the results. It has long lines and zero atmosphere, but who cares when faced with a Ferdi special—a giant roll filled with baked ham, roast beef, gravy, and debris (the bits of beef that fall off when the roast is carved). There's other food, including one of the best breakfasts in the city, but the po' boys are what New Orleans goes for, and you should, too. Mother's is within walking distance of the Louisiana Superdome and a number of major hotels. Be sure to allow time to stand in line. It usually moves quickly, and there's always a seat when you get your food.

✪ **Uglesich's Restaurant & Bar.** 1238 Barrone St. ☎ **504/523-8571.** Reservations not accepted. Menu items $9–$13. No credit cards. Mon–Fri 9am–4pm, open every other Sat (seasonal). SANDWICHES/SEAFOOD.

It's dangerous to call any one place "the best in New Orleans," but it's mighty tempting to make an exception for "Ugly's," a tiny, crowded, greasy neighborhood place that serves some of the most divine seafood in town. At lunch time, especially during busy tourist times, you might have a very long wait before you order at the counter, another wait for a table, and a third wait for your food. But we swear it will be worth it. Obviously, others who should know think so; you might well end up sitting next to some of the best chefs in town, because this is where *they* go for lunch. (Although you might just want to skip Uglesich's altogether during Jazz Fest and Mardi Gras time. If you do go, at least bring a book or a bunch of chatty friends. During a recent Jazz Fest visit, the wait took from $2^1/_2$ to—get this—*4 hours.* Even dedicated fans find it hard to justify that sort of time commitment.)

It's hard to narrow down the dishes, even as it's hard to try new ones when you really want to keep eating splendid old favorites. Among the musts are fried green tomatoes with shrimp rémoulade, shrimp in creamy sauce on a fried cake of grits, voodoo shrimp (in a peppery butter sauce), and trout all kinds of ways. Order extra bread to sop up sauce, but be sure to ask for it unbuttered. You'll be full, you might smell of grease, and you might well come back for more the next day.

5 Uptown/Garden District

EXPENSIVE

✪ **Brigtsen's.** 723 Dante St. ☎ **504/861-7610.** Reservations required (a week or 2 in advance). Main courses $14–$28; 3-course "Early Evening" dinner (Tues–Thurs 5:30–6:30pm) $14.95. AE, DC, MC, V. Tues–Sat 5:30–10pm. CAJUN/CREOLE.

In a setting both elegant and homey, chef Frank Brigsten serves some of the city's best contemporary Creole cuisine. Nestled in a converted 19th-century house at the Riverbend, Brigtsen's is a warm, intimate, and romantic. The individual dining rooms are small and cozy, and the menu changes daily. Brigsten has a special touch with rabbit; one of his most mouth-watering dishes is an appetizer of rabbit tenderloin on a tasso Parmesan grits cake, with sautéed spinach and a Creole mustard sauce. The rabbit and andouille gumbo is delicious, intensely flavored, and well balanced. You can't miss with any of the soups, especially the lovely butternut squash shrimp bisque, and there's an entree to please everyone. One of the most popular dishes is roast duck with cornbread dressing and pecan gravy, with the duck skin roasted to a delightful crackle. We enjoyed the broiled fish of the day (sheep's head on a recent visit) with crabmeat Parmesan crust and a delicate, tangy lemon mousseline sauce, and pan-roasted drum fish topped with lots of lump crabmeat and chanterelle mushrooms, surrounded by a wonderful crab broth. Save room for dessert, including the signature banana bread pudding with banana rum sauce. Brigsten's offers one of the loveliest evenings you'll spend in a Crescent City restaurant. And the "Early Evening" dinner special is as good a bargain as you'll find.

✪ **Commander's Palace.** 1403 Washington Ave. ☎ **504/899-8221.** Reservations required. Jackets required at night and Sun brunch; no shorts, T-shirts, tennis shoes, blue jeans. Main courses $29–$32; full brunch $20–$32; fixed-price $29–$36. AE, CB, DC, DISC, MC, V. Mon–Fri 11:30am–1:30pm, Sat 11:30am–12:30pm, Sun brunch 10:30am–1:30pm; daily 6–9:30pm. CREOLE.

Voted the best restaurant in the United States—that's right, in the whole country—by the James Beard Foundation in 1996, Commander's is one place that lives up to its reputation. (And recently, the Foundation gave it their Lifetime Outstanding Restaurant award.) It's not just the food—which is never less than good— it's the whole package. In a beautiful 1880s Victorian house, it consists of a nearly endless series of dining rooms, from large to intimate, each more appealing and romantic than the last. On balmy nights, you can eat in the lovely courtyard. (A somewhat less desirable modern dining room is in the back—try to skip that one, if you can.) The wait staff is incredibly attentive; several people pamper you throughout your meal. Each night features a multicourse fixed-price menu for around $35, with evening specialties. It also allows you to mix and match off the regular menu—a good bargain and a great splurge.

The famous turtle soup with sherry is outstanding, so thick it's nearly a stew. Don't miss it. Other marvelous appetizer choices include the shrimp and tasso with five pepper jelly, carpaccio salad with roasted eggplant garlic and the hearty crawfish bisque with homemade biscuits. Main course selections change seasonally, but you are best off sticking with Creole-type offerings, such as the frequently available dreamy boned Mississippi roasted quail stuffed with Creole crawfish sausage, the Mississippi rabbit with a sauté of onions, turnips, mushrooms and concasse tomatoes topped with rabbit consommé and pastry shell, or the mixed grill (including lamb and rabbit sausage!) rather than, say, more nouvelle-cuisine such as ultimately bland panfried fish. Your serving team will tell you to try the famous bread pudding soufflé. Trust them. But all the desserts are exceptional; chocolate lovers should not overlook the chocolate Sheba, a sort of solid chocolate mousse, ever so slightly chilled, covered in nuts. And everyone should consider the Creole Cream Cheesecake, which will make you rethink your position on cheesecakes. Then there is the gorgeous rendition of pecan pie à la mode, and the not-on-the-menu-so-ask-for-it Chocolate Molten Souffle. There's an excellent wine list, and the menu offers suggestions with each entree. This is one must-do New Orleans restaurant, particularly appropriate for special occasions—but you can simply call your trip to New Orleans a special occasion, and we won't tell.

Mike's on the Avenue. In the Lafayette Hotel, 628 St. Charles Ave. ☎ **504/523-1709.** Reservations recommended. Main courses $9–$15 at lunch, $16–$30 at dinner. AE, DC, DISC, MC, V. Daily 7–10am and 6–10pm; Mon–Fri 11:30am–2pm. NEW AMERICAN/INTERNATIONAL.

On the ground floor of the Lafayette Hotel, Mike's on the Avenue has become extremely popular with New Orleanians over the past few years. It's a fun, interesting place, right on the Avenue indeed (what a place to watch a Mardi Gras parade, with those broad expanses of windows looking out at St. Charles), the walls covered in canvases painted by the chef himself. The food is Asian-influenced and clever ("East meets SouthWest New Orleans" and "perfection through spontaneous imperfection" is how they describe it), not as heavy as in many places in town, but doesn't always hit the mark as strongly as one might like. Skip the tasty-sounding sampler platter in favor of the best dish on it, the Chinese shrimp dumplings. Fish dishes can be quite spicy, while vegetarians will be pleased with the noodle pillo, a concoction of angel hair pasta, stir-fried vegetables and teriyaki glaze. Desserts are quite good, particularly the Wabi Tower, a spiral of dark chocolate filled with chocolate truffle cream, fresh raspberries and devil's food cake, with a white chocolate sauce.

☯ Upperline. 1413 Upperline St. ☎ **504/891-9822.** Reservations required. Main courses $16.50–$24. AE, CB, DC, MC, V. Sun brunch 11:30am–2pm; Wed–Sun 5:30–9:30pm. ECLECTIC/CREOLE.

In a small, charming house in a largely residential area, the Upperline is more low key than high-profile places such as Emeril's. In its own way, though, it's every bit as inventive. It's a great place to try imaginative food at reasonable (by fancy restaurant standards) prices. Owner JoAnn Clevenger and her staff are quite friendly, and their attitude is reflected in the part of the menu where they actually—gasp!—recommend dishes at *other* restaurants. Perhaps you can afford to be so generous when your own offerings are so strong. Standout appetizers include their fried green tomatoes with shrimp rémoulade sauce (they invented this dish, which is now featured just about everywhere in town), spicy shrimp on jalapeño corn bread, duck confit, and fried sweetbreads. For entrees, there's moist, herb-crusted pork loin, roast duck with a sauce that tingles, and a fall-off-the-bone lamb shank. If you're lucky, there will be a special menu, like the all-garlic selection, where even dessert contains garlic. For dessert, try warm honey-pecan bread pudding or chocolate hazelnut mousse. The award-winning wine list focuses primarily on California selections.

MODERATE

Gautreau's. 1728 Soniat St. ☎ **504/899-7397.** Reservations recommended. Main courses $14–$28. AE, DC, DISC, MC, V. Mon–Sat 6–10pm. INTERNATIONAL.

Those who knew the old Gautreau's (which closed in 1989 and reopened under new ownership) will be relieved to see that the restaurant has retained its warm and modest decor: The tin ceiling, the old New Orleans photographs, and the famous apothecary cabinet from the original drugstore have all been retained. The quality of the food has not changed, either. Rob Mitchell, a graduate of the Culinary Institute of America, has worked at Gautreau's since 1993 and became the head chef in 1995. Menus change seasonally; if you spot them on the menu, try the marinated shrimp and Dungeness crab, served with sticky rice and orange-and-honey soy sauce, or warm crisped duck confit with sherried flageolets, mustard, and sage. Recent favorite entrees include sautéed tilapia and shrimp with basmati rice, arugula, and chile mango sauce, and roasted chicken with wild mushrooms, garlic potatoes, and green beans. The pastry chef does a fine honey-orange crème brûlée and a delightful triple-layer (chocolate, maple pecan, and almond) cheesecake.

Kelsey's. 3923 Magazine St. ☎ **504/897-6722.** Reservations recommended. Main courses $6.95–$12.95 at lunch, $12.95–$24.95 at dinner. AE, DC, DISC, MC, V. Tues–Fri 11:30am–2pm; Tues–Thurs 5:30–9:30pm, Fri–Sat 5:30–10pm. CREOLE.

For nearly 5 years, Kelsey's lay hidden on the east bank of the Mississippi River in Algiers, known only to loyal patrons and restaurant critics. Then, in 1996, co-owners Randy and Ina Barlow moved

Kelsey's to uptown New Orleans. The new space's light colors and attentive servers make the atmosphere nearly serene.

For 8 years Randy Barlow worked at K-Paul's with Paul Prudhomme, and the influence is apparent. The house specialty is eggplant Kelsey, a batter-fried eggplant pirogue (in the shape of a boat) stuffed with seafood seasoned with Parmesan and Romano cheeses, tomatoes, garlic, olive oil, parsley and lemon juice. Many dishes are equally elaborate, but Barlow can also make the simple stuff shine. Especially enjoyable are the tomato-and-provolone salad, a lightly panfried Gulf fish special, and apple raspberry crisp with fresh cream. There's a well-chosen selection of wines by the glass.

Pascal's Manale. 1838 Napoleon Ave. ☎ **504/895-4877.** Reservations recommended. Main courses $13.95–$22. AE, CB, DC, DISC, MC, V. Year-round Mon–Fri 11:30am–10pm, Sat 4–10pm. ITALIAN/STEAK/SEAFOOD.

Barbecued shrimp. This restaurant has made its reputation with that one dish, and you should go there if only for that. The place is crowded and noisy and verges on expensive, but it grows on you. Don't expect fancy decor—the emphasis is on food and conviviality. (Sunday nights especially feel like social gatherings.) Pascal's bills itself as an Italian–New Orleans steak house, but the presence of such specialties as veal Marsala, turtle soup, the combination pan roast, and those barbecued shrimp (a house creation) give the menu a decidedly idiosyncratic slant. By "barbecued," we don't mean on a grill, but in a rich, spicy, buttery sauce that demands that you soak up every drop with as much bread as you can get out of your waiter. Try not to think about your arteries too much; vow to walk your socks off tomorrow, lick your fingers, and enjoy.

INEXPENSIVE

✪ **Camellia Grill.** 626 S. Carrollton Ave. ☎ **504/866-9573.** Reservations not accepted. All items under $10. No credit cards. Mon–Thurs 9am–1am, Fri 9am–3am, Sat 8am–3am, Sun 8am–1am. HAMBURGERS/SANDWICHES.

Even though it's *only* been a part of New Orleans' food culture since 1946, the Camellia Grill seems to have always been there. Right off the St. Charles Avenue streetcar, it's a fixture in many people's lives. As you sit on a stool at the double-U shaped counter, white-jacketed waiters pamper you while shouting cryptic orders to the chefs. There's often a wait, because the Camellia serves some of the best breakfasts and burgers anywhere, but the wait is always worth it. The Camellia is famous for its omelettes—heavy and fluffy at the same time, and almost as big as a rolled-up newspaper. Notable choices are the chili cheese and the potato, onion, and cheese (a personal favorite). Don't forget the pecan waffle, a moan-inducing work of art. If you're feeling really decadent, go with a friend, order omelettes, and split a waffle on the side. The burgers are big and sloppy and among the best in town. Wash it all down with one of the famous chocolate freezes, then contemplate a slice of the celebrated pie for dessert (the chocolate pecan may be to die for).

✪ **Casamento's.** 4330 Magazine St. ☎ **504/895-9761.** Reservations not accepted. Main courses $4.95–$11. No credit cards. Tues–Sun 11:30am–1:30pm and 5:30–9pm. Closed mid-June to mid-Sept. SEAFOOD.

This restaurant takes oysters so seriously that it just closes down when they're not in season. It pays off—this is *the* oyster place. You pay a bit more for a dozen, but your reward is a presentation that shows the care the staff puts in; the oysters are more cleanly scrubbed and well selected. You might also take the plunge and order an oyster loaf: a big, fat loaf of bread fried in butter, filled with oysters (or shrimp), and fried again to seal it. Do your arteries a favor and only eat half (though your stomach might demand the whole thing!). Casamento's also has terrific gumbo—perhaps the best in town. It's small (you have to walk through the kitchen to get to the rest rooms), but the atmosphere is light, with the waitresses serving up jokes and poking good-natured fun at you, at each other, or at the guys behind the oyster bar.

Figaro's Pizzeria. 7900 Maple St. ☎ **504/866-0100.** Reservations not accepted. Pizzas $6.50–$16.25; sandwiches and main courses $5.25–$9.75. AE, DC, DISC, MC, V. Mon–Thurs 11:30am–10:30pm, Fri–Sat 11:30am–11:30pm, Sun 11:30am–10pm. PIZZA/ITALIAN.

A few blocks uptown from Tulane University, Figaro's draws a semicasual crowd looking for designer pizza, cosmopolitan Italian food, and a nice outdoor patio for watching the beautiful people. Among the Neopolitan-style pies, spinach and feta is a personal favorite, but there are plenty of others from which to choose. How about a white pizza with garlic-herb butter and mozzarella, one with shrimp and cilantro, or the Margherita, with tomatoes and basil. You can also create an American-style pizza to your taste or make a meal of a calzone, an antipasto salad, a sub sandwich, or a muffaletta. I recommend any of the pasta entrees, especially the Sicilian stuffed shells. This is a good stop if you're at the university or in the Audubon Park area, especially if the weather is right for lunch outside.

Mystic Cafe. 3244 Magazine St. ☎ **504/891-1992.** Main courses $5.75–$11.25. AE, DISC, MC, V. Sun–Thurs 11am–11pm, Fri–Sat 11am–midnight. MEDITERRANEAN.

Local vegetarians flock here, though the cafe is technically Mediterranean (which means anything from Italy to Turkey), and some dishes include meat. The food is mostly butter-free and can be made without sugar on request. Vegans and the heart-conscious will find plenty of whole-grain, high-quality olive oil options. Some might find it a welcome relief from the usual full-fat New Orleans diet, but others might feel they are dining in California. That's fine for California, but not for New Orleans.

6 Metairie

Bozo's. 3117 21st St. ☎ **504/831-8666.** Lunch $5–$10; dinner $12–$16. MC, V. Tues–Sat 11am–3pm; Tues–Thurs 5–10pm, Fri–Sat 5–11pm. CAJUN/SEAFOOD.

New Orleanians have much affection for this plain, unpretentious fish house, and it's easy to see why, when the friendly and efficient wait staff serves heaping plates of seafood cooked to perfection. Shrimp, oysters, crawfish, crabs, and almost anything that swims or lives in nearby waters make up the bulk of the menu. Try the crisp and utterly delectable fried catfish lightly breaded with cornmeal, or "Mama Bozo's" delectable chicken andouille gumbo. There are a few other non-seafood selections, and a good list of sandwiches. Prices are unbelievably low, starting with a bargain gumbo and topping out with rib-eye steak. It's worth the trip.

Crozier's Restaurant Français. 3216 W. Esplanade North. ☎ **504/833-8108.** Reservations recommended. Main courses $16.25–$21. AE, DC, DISC, MC, V. Tues–Sat 5:30–10pm. FRENCH.

Authentic French cooking accounts for this restaurant's longstanding popularity. There are no surprises here, just good, old-fashioned French cuisine that would make any native (particularly from the south of France, like chef Gerard Crozier) feel right at home. Begin with a very tasty traditional onion soup or a salad of mixed greens. There's also a nice duck liver pâté and, of course, the ever-present escargots. Entrees might include trout with pecans, fish du jour, steak au poivre, or an incredible grilled quail with a light demi-glace. Traditional desserts like crème caramel, mousse au chocolat, and various tartlettes are a nice way to finish a meal. The wine list is limited, but good and moderately priced.

7 Coffee, Tea & Sweets

✪ **Café du Monde.** In the French Market, 813 Decatur St. ☎ **504/581-2914.** Coffee, milk, hot chocolate, and beignets $1.10. No credit cards. Daily 24 hrs. Closed Dec 25. COFFEE, TEA & SWEETS.

Excuse us while we wax rhapsodic. Since 1862, Café du Monde has been selling café au lait and beignets on the edge of Jackson Square. A New Orleans landmark, it's *the* place for people-watching. Not only is it a must-stop on any trip to New Orleans, but you may find yourself wandering back several times a day, for your morning beignet and coffee, your afternoon snack, and, best of all, your 3am pick-me-up. What's a beignet? (Say ben-*yay*, by the way.) A square French doughnut-type object, hot and covered in powdered sugar. You might be tempted to shake off some of the sugar. Don't. Trust us. Pour more on, even. You'll be glad you did. Just don't wear black, or everyone will know what you've been eating. At three for about $1, they're a hell of a deal. Wash them down with chicory coffee, listen to the nearby buskers, ignore people trying to get your table, and try to figure out how many more stops you can squeeze in during your visit.

Kaldi's Coffeehouse and Museum. 941 Decatur St. ☎ **504/586-8989.** Sun–Thurs 7am–midnight, Fri–Sat 7am–2am. COFFEE, TEA & SWEETS.

Local alterna-youths and folkies come to this high-ceilinged, airy spot to brood over their journals and swig all kinds of coffee drinks. The menu is quite long and features everything from the traditional to the trendy (mocha drinks and whatnot) to the vaguely healthful (the blended soy drink is surprisingly tasty). They even roast the coffee beans on the premises. Poetry readings and folk music sometimes happen at night. This is a good place to drop by, not just for the addictive drinks, but also to find out what's happening in underground and alternative New Orleans.

6

Sights to See & Places to Be

*N*ow, we admit that our favorite New Orleans activities involve walking, eating, listening to music, and dancing. If that's all you do while in town, we won't complain. Still, some people feel guilty if they don't take in some culture or history while on vacation. And besides, frequently you need to escape the rain or heat. New Orleans offers several fine museums and a world-class aquarium and zoo, all of which, in addition to being interesting in and of themselves, make marvelous refuges from the weather (except perhaps for the zoo).

Frankly, New Orleans itself is one big sight. It's one of the most unusual-looking cities in America, and being nice and flat, it's just made for exploring on foot. So get out there and do so. Be sure not to confine yourself to the French Quarter. While it certainly is a seductive place, to go to New Orleans and never leave the Quarter is like going to New York, remaining in Greenwich Village, and believing you've seen Manhattan. Stroll the lush Garden District or marvel at the oaks in City Park. Ride the streetcar down St. Charles Avenue and gape with jealousy at the gorgeous homes. Get really active and go visit some gators on a swamp tour.

1 The French Quarter

Those who have been to Disneyland might be forgiven if they experience some déjà vu upon first seeing the French Quarter. It's somewhat more worn, of course, and, in spots, a whole lot smellier. But it's also real. However, thanks perhaps in part to Disney, many tourists treat the Quarter like a theme park, going from bar to bar instead of ride to ride, broadcasting their every move with rowdy shrieks of merriment.

Fine. Except it isn't an amusement park, constructed just for the hedonistic delight of out-of-towners. It's an actual neighborhood, one of the most visually interesting in America and one that has existed for more than 200 years. Some of the people living in the Quarter are the fifth generation of their family to do so.

Aside from Bourbon Street, you will find the most bustling activity at **Jackson Square,** where musicians, artists, fortune-tellers,

French Quarter Attractions

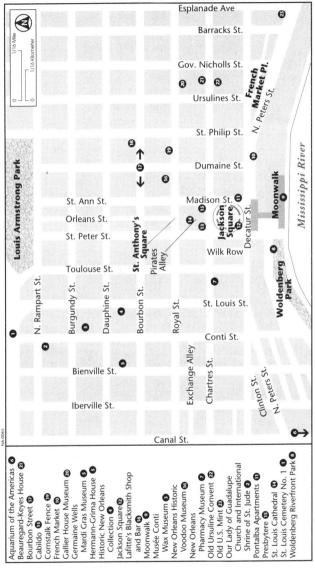

Aquarium of the Americas **6**
Beauregard-Keyes House **21**
Bourbon Street **7**
Cabildo **13**
Cornstalk Fence **19**
French Market **10**
Gallier House Museum **20**
Germaine Wells
Mardi Gras Museum **5**
Hermann-Grima House **4**
Historic New Orleans
Collection **4**
Jackson Square **12**
Lafitte's Blacksmith Shop
and Bar **18**
Moonwalk **9**
Musée Conti
Wax Museum **3**
New Orleans Historic
Voodoo Museum **16**
New Orleans
Pharmacy Museum **7**
Old Ursuline Convent **22**
Old U.S. Mint **23**
Our Lady of Guadalupe
Church and International
Shrine of St. Jude **2**
Pontalba Apartments **11**
Presbytere **15**
St. Louis Cathedral **14**
St. Louis Cemetery No. 1 **1**
Woldenberg Riverfront Park **8**

NA-0065

87

jugglers, and those peculiar "living statue" performance artists (a step below mime, and that's pretty pathetic) gather, to sell their wares or entertain for change. **Royal Street** is home to numerous pricey antique shops, with other interesting stores on **Chartres and Decatur streets** and the cross streets between.

The closer you get to Esplanade Avenue and toward Rampart Street, the more residential the Quarter becomes, and buildings are entirely homes (in the business sections, the ground floors are commercial and the stories above apartments). Walk through these areas, peeping in through any open gate; surprises wait behind them in the form of graceful brick and flagstone-lined courtyards filled with foliage and bubbling fountains.

Though much of New Orleans is made for walking, the Quarter is particularly pedestrian-friendly. The streets are laid out in an almost perfect rectangle, so it's nearly impossible to get lost. It's also so well traveled that it is nearly always safe, particularly in the central parts. Again, as you get toward the fringes (especially near Rampart) and as night falls, you should exercise caution; stay in the more bustling parts and try not to walk alone.

✪ **Aquarium of the Americas.** 1 Canal St., at Wells St. ☎ **800/774-7394** or 504/581-4629. www.auduboninstitute.org. Aquarium $11.25 adults, $8.75 seniors, $5 children 2–12. IMAX $7.75 adults, $6.75 seniors, $5 children. Combination tickets $15.50 adults, $12.50 seniors, $9 children. Aquarium Sun–Thurs 9:30am–6pm, Fri–Sat 9:30am–7pm. IMAX daily 10am–6pm. Shows every hour on the hour. Last ticket sold 1 hour before closing. Closed Mardi Gras and Dec 25.

With all the other delights New Orleans offers, it's easy to overlook the Audubon Institute's Aquarium of the Americas—despite its million-gallon size. Who wants to look at fish when you could be eating them? But this is a world-class aquarium, highly entertaining and painlessly educational, with beautifully constructed exhibits.

The Aquarium is on the banks of the Mississippi River, along Woldenberg Park at the edge of the French Quarter—a very easy walk from the main Quarter action. Five major exhibit areas and dozens of smaller aquariums hold a veritable ocean of aquatic life native to the region (especially the Mississippi River and Gulf of Mexico) and to North, Central, and South America. You can walk through the underwater tunnel in the Caribbean Reef exhibit and wave to finny friends swimming all around you, view a shark-filled re-creation of the Gulf of Mexico, or drop in to see the penguin exhibit. We particularly like the walk-through Waters of the

Americas, where you wander in rain forests (complete with birds and piranhas) and see what goes on below the surface of swamps; one look will squash any thoughts of a dip in a bayou. *Note:* At press time, plans were being made for a sea otter exhibit.

The IMAX theater shows two or three films at regular intervals. The Aquarium is a great place to take the kids, though most will probably be too impatient to learn much from the educational graphics. And adults shouldn't overlook it, even if you are inclined to think it isn't your, er, bowl of chowder. In addition to its many virtues, it also makes a perfect refuge from the inevitable rain.

The Audubon Institute also runs the city's zoo at Audubon Park uptown. Combination tickets for the Aquarium, the IMAX theater, the zoo, and a riverboat ride to the zoo are $26.50 for adults, $13.25 for children. You can also buy tickets for different combinations of the attractions.

The Historic French Market. On Decatur St., toward Esplanade Ave. from Jackson Sq.

Legend has it that the site of the French Market was originally used by Native Americans as a bartering market. It began to grow into an official market in 1812. Circa 1840-70, it was part of Gallatin Street, an impossibly rough area so full of bars, drunken sailors, and criminals of every shape and size that it made Bourbon Street look like Disneyland. Today, it's a mixed bag (and not nearly as colorful as its past). The 24-hour Farmer's Market makes a fun amble as you admire everything from fresh produce and fish to more tourist-oriented items like hot sauces, Cajun and Creole mixes, and snacks like gator on a stick (when was the last time you had that?). The Flea Market, a bit farther down from the Farmer's Market, is considered a must-shop place, but the reality is that the goods are kind of junky: T-shirts, jewelry, hats, belts, crystals, sunglasses, and that sort of thing. Still, some good deals are to be had (even better if you are up for bargaining), so the savvy might find it the right place for souvenir shopping. The flea market is open daily.

St. Louis Cathedral. 721 Chartres St. ☎ **504/525-9585.** Free admission. Free tours run continuously Mon–Sat 9am–5pm, Sun 2–5pm.

The St. Louis Cathedral prides itself on being the oldest continuously active cathedral in the United States. What usually doesn't get mentioned is that it is also one of the ugliest. The outside is all right, but the rather grim interior wouldn't give even a minor European church a run for its money.

·Still, its history is impressive and somewhat dramatic. The cathedral formed the center of the original settlement, and it is still the major landmark of the French Quarter. This is the third building to stand on this spot. A hurricane destroyed the first in 1722. On Good Friday 1788, the bells of its replacement were kept silent for religious reasons rather than ringing out the alarm for a fire—which eventually went out of control and burned down more than 850 buildings, including the cathedral itself.

Rebuilt in 1794, the structure was remodeled and enlarged between 1845 and 1851 by J. N. B. de Pouilly. It's of Spanish design, with a tower at each end and a higher central tower. The brick used in its construction was taken from the original town cemetery and covered with stucco to protect the mortar from dampness. It's worth going in to catch one of the free docent tours; the knowledgeable guides are full of fun facts about the windows and murals and how the building nearly collapsed once from water table sinkage. Be sure to look at the slope of the floor; clever architectural design somehow keeps the building upright even as it continues to sink.

HISTORIC BUILDINGS

Old Absinthe House. 240 Bourbon St., between Iberville and Bienville. ☎ **504/523-3181.** Free admission. Daily from 9:30am.

The Old Absinthe House was built in 1806 by two Spaniards and is still owned by their descendants (who live in Spain and have nothing to do with running the place). The building now houses the Old Absinthe House bar and two restaurants, Tony Moran's and Pasta E Vino. The drink for which the building and bar were named is now outlawed in this country (it only caused blindness and madness). But you can sip a legal libation in the bar and feel at one with the famous types who came before you, listed on a plaque outside: William Makepeace Thackeray, Oscar Wilde, Sarah Bernhardt, Walt Whitman. Andrew Jackson and the Lafitte brothers plotted their desperate defense of New Orleans here in 1815. The house was a speakeasy during Prohibition, and when federal officers closed it in 1924, the interior was mysteriously stripped of its antique fixtures—including the long marble-topped bar and the old water dripper that was used to infuse water into the absinthe. Just as mysteriously, they all reappeared down the street at a corner establishment called, oddly enough, the Old Absinthe House Bar (400 Bourbon St.). The latter recently closed, and a neon-bedecked daiquiri shack opened in its stead. Needless to say, the fixtures are nowhere in sight.

Beauregard–Keyes House. 1113 Chartres St., at Ursulines. ☎ **504/523-7257.** Admission $5 adults, $4 seniors and students and AAA, $1.50 children under 13. Mon–Sat 10am–3pm. Tours on the hour.

This "raised cottage," with its Doric columns and handsome twin staircases, was built as a residence by a wealthy New Orleans auctioneer, Joseph Le Carpentier, in 1826. Confederate Gen. P. G. T. Beauregard lived in the house with several members of his family for 18 months between 1865 and 1867, and from 1944 until 1970 it was the residence of Frances Parkinson Keyes (pronounced *Cause*), who wrote many novels about the region. One of them, *Madame Castel's Lodger,* concerns the general's stay in this house. *Dinner at Antoine's,* perhaps her most famous novel, also was written here. Mrs. Keyes left her home to a foundation, and the house, rear buildings, and garden are open to the public. The gift shop has a wide selection of her novels.

Old Ursuline Convent. 1112 Chartres St., at Ursuline. ☎ **504/529-3040.** Admission $5 adults, $4 seniors, $2 students, free for children under 8. Tours Tues–Fri 10am–3pm on the hour (closed for lunch at noon), Sat–Sun 11:15am, 1, and 2pm.

Forget tales of America being founded by brawny, brave tough guys in buckskin and beards. The real pioneers—at least, in Louisiana—were well-educated French women clad in 40 pounds of black wool robes. That's right; you don't know tough until you know the Ursuline nuns, and this city would have been a very different place without them. The Sisters of Ursula came to the mudhole that was New Orleans in 1727, after enduring a journey that several times nearly saw them lost at sea or to pirates or disease. Once in town, they provided the first decent medical care (saving countless lives), and later, founded the local first school and orphanage for girls. They also helped raise girls shipped over from France as marriage material for local men, teaching the girls everything from languages to homemaking of the most exacting sort (laying the foundation for who knows how many local families). The Convent dates from 1752 (the Sisters themselves moved uptown in 1824, where they remain to this day) and is the oldest building in the Mississippi River Valley, and the only surviving building from the French Colonial period in the United States. It also houses Catholic archives dating back to 1718. Unfortunately, tours here can be disappointing affairs, with docents whose histories ramble all over the place, rarely painting the full, thrilling picture of these extraordinary ladies to whom New Orleans owes so much.

The Old U.S. Mint. 400 Esplanade Ave., at N. Peters (enter on Esplanade Ave. or Barracks St.). ☎ **800/568-6968** or 504/568-6968. Admission $5 adults, $4 seniors and students, free for children under 12. Tues–Sun 9am–5pm.

The Old U.S. Mint, a Louisiana State Museum complex, houses exhibits on New Orleans jazz and on the city's Carnival celebrations. The first exhibit contains a comprehensive collection of pictures, musical instruments, and other artifacts connected with jazz greats— Louis Armstrong's first trumpet is here. It tells of the development of the jazz tradition and New Orleans' place in that history. Across the hall there's a stunning array of Carnival mementos from New Orleans and other communities across Louisiana—from ornate Mardi Gras costumes to a street scene complete with maskers and a parade float. The Krewe of Zulu, one of the city's most festive Mardi Gras societies, donated costumes from years past that recently went on display.

The 1850 House, Lower Pontalba Building. 523 St. Ann St., Jackson Sq. ☎ **504/568-6968.** Admission $3 adults, $2 seniors and students, free for children under 13. Tues–Sun 9am–5pm. Closed state holidays.

James Gallier Sr. and his son designed the historic Pontalba Buildings for the Baroness Micaela Almonester de Pontalba. She had them built in 1849 in an effort to combat the deterioration of the older part of the city. The rows of town houses on either side of Jackson Square were the largest private buildings in the country at the time. Legend has it that the Baroness, miffed that her friend Andrew Jackson wouldn't tip his hat to her, had his statue erected in the square, permanently doffing his chapeau toward her apartment on the top floor of the Upper Pontalba. It's probably not true, but we never stand in the way of a good story.

In this house, the Louisiana State Museum presents a demonstration of life in 1850, when the buildings opened for residential use. The self-guided tour uses a fact-filled sheet that explains in detail the history of the interior and the uses of the rooms, which are filled with period furnishings arranged to show how the rooms were typically used. It vividly illustrates the difference between the "upstairs" portion of the house, where the upper middle-class family lived in comfort (and the children were largely confined to a nursery and raised by servants), and the "downstairs," where the staff toiled in considerable drudgery to make their bosses comfortable. It's a surprisingly enjoyable look at life in the "good old days"; it might have you reconsidering just how good they were.

Spring Fiesta Historic House. 826 St. Ann St., at Bourbon. ☎ **504/581-1367.** $4 donation requested. By appointment only.

The New Orleans Spring Fiesta Association owns this historic mid–19th-century town house. It affords a peek back in time, furnished as it is with antiques of the Victorian era and many objets d'art from New Orleans' golden age of the 1800s. The association's fiesta, in March, coordinates tours of historic town houses, courtyards, and plantation homes around the city.

MUSEUMS

In addition to the destinations listed here, you might be interested in the **Germaine Wells Mardi Gras Museum** (☎ **504/523-5433**), 813 Bienville St., on the second floor of Arnaud's restaurant. You'll find a private collection of Mardi Gras costumes and ball gowns dating from around 1910 to 1960. Admission is free, and the museum is open during restaurant hours. **The Old U.S. Mint** (see "Historic Buildings," above) displays a few Mardi Gras costumes, and also houses a collection of jazz memorabilia.

Scheduled to open in 2000 are the **National D-Day Museum,** a tribute to those who made the Normandy invasion possible; and the **Ogden Museum of Southern Art.**

✪ **The Cabildo.** 701 Chartres St. ☎ **504/568-6968.** Admission $5 adults, $4 students and seniors, free for children under 13. Tues–Sun 9am–5pm.

Constructed in 1795–99 as the Spanish government seat in New Orleans, the Cabildo was the site of the signing of the Louisiana Purchase transfer. It was severely damaged by fire in 1988, and closed for 5 years for reconstruction, which included total restoration of the roof by French artisans using 600-year-old timber-framing techniques. It is now the center of the Louisiana State Museum's facilities in the French Quarter. It's conveniently located right there on Jackson Square and is quite worth your time.

A multiroom exhibition informatively, entertainingly, and exhaustively traces the history of Louisiana from exploration through Reconstruction, from a multicultural perspective. It covers all aspects of life, not just the obvious discussions of slavery and the battle for statehood. Topics include antebellum music, mourning and burial customs (a big deal when much of your population is succumbing to yellow fever), immigrants and how they fared here, and the changing roles of women in the South (which occupies a large space). As you wander through, each room seems more interesting than the last. Throughout are portraits of nearly all the prominent figures from Louisiana history, plus other fabulous artifacts, including Napoléon's death mask.

Gallier House Museum. 1118 and 1132 Royal St., between Gov. Nicholls and Ursuline sts. ☎ **504/525-5661.** Admission $6 adults, $5.25 AAA members, $5 seniors and students, $3 children 8–18, free for children under 8. Tours begin on the half hour Mon–Sat 10am–4pm; last tour at 3:30pm.

James Gallier Jr. designed and built the Gallier House Museum as his residence in 1857. Anne Rice fans will want to at least walk by, because this is the house she was thinking of when she described Louis and Lestat's New Orleans residence in *Interview with the Vampire.* Gallier and his father were leading New Orleans architects—they designed the old French Opera House, the original St. Charles Exchange Hotel, Municipality Hall (now Gallier Hall), and the Pontalba Buildings. This carefully restored town house contains an early working bathroom, a passive ventilation system, and furnishings of the period. Leaders of local ghost tours swear Gallier haunts the place. The adjoining building houses historical exhibits as well as films on decorative plasterwork, ornamental ironwork, woodgraining, and marbling. There is also a gift shop and plenty of free parking. Special seasonal programs are available.

Hermann-Grima House. 820 St. Louis St. ☎ **504/525-5661.** Admission $6 adults, $5.25 AAA members, $5 seniors and students, $3 children 8–18, free for children under 8. Mon–Sat 10am–4pm (last tour leaves at 3:30pm).

Brought to you by the same folks who run the Gallier House, the 1831 Hermann-Grima House is a symmetrical Federal-style building (perhaps the first in the Quarter) that's very different from its French surroundings. The knowledgeable docents who give the regular tours make this a satisfactory stop at any time, but keep an eye out for the frequent special tours. At Halloween, for example, the house is draped in typical 1800s mourning, and the docents explain mourning customs; at Christmas, the house and tour reflect that season. The house, which stretches from St. Louis Street to Conti Street, passed through two different families before becoming a boarding house in the 1920s. It has been meticulously restored and researched, and the tour is one of the city's more historically accurate offerings. On Thursdays from October to May, cooking demonstrations take place in the authentic 1830s kitchen, using methods of the era. (Alas, health rules prevent those on the tour from sampling the results.) The house also contains one of the Quarter's last surviving stables, complete with stalls.

✪ **Historic New Orleans Collection—Museum/Research Center.** 533 Royal St. (between St. Louis and Toulouse). ☎ **504/523-4662.** Free admission; tours $4. Tues–Sat 10am–4:45pm; tours Tues–Sat 10am, 11am, 2pm, 3pm. Closed major holidays, Mardi Gras.

The Historic New Orleans Collection's museum of local and regional history is almost hidden away within a complex of historic French Quarter buildings. The oldest, constructed in the late 18th century, was one of the few structures to escape the disastrous fire of 1794. These buildings were owned by the collection's founders, Gen. and Mrs. L. Kemper Williams. Their former residence, behind the courtyard, is open to the public for tours. There are also excellent tours of the Louisiana history galleries, which feature choice items from the collection—expertly preserved and displayed art, maps, and original documents like the transfer papers for the Louisiana Purchase of 1803. The collection is owned and managed by a private foundation, not a governmental organization, and therefore offers more historical perspective and artifacts than boosterism. The Williams Gallery, also on the site, is free to the public and presents changing exhibitions that focus on Louisiana's history and culture.

If you want to see another grandly restored French Quarter building (and a researcher's dream), visit the **Williams Research Center,** 410 Chartres St. (☎ **504/598-7171**), which houses and displays the bulk of the collection's many thousands of items. Admission is free.

Madame John's Legacy. 632 Dumaine Street. ☎ **504/568-6968.** Admission $3 adults, $2 students and seniors. Tues–Sun 9am–5pm.

The second oldest building in the Mississippi Valley (after the Ursuline Convent), and a rare example of Creole architecture that miraculously survived the 1794 fire, Madame John's Legacy has finally been opened to the public. Built around 1788, on the foundations of an earlier home destroyed in the fire of that year, the house has had a number of owners and renters (including the son of Governor Claiborne), but none of them were named John. Or even Madame. It acquired its moniker courtesy of author George Washington Cable, who used the house as a setting for his short story "Tite Poulette." The protagonist was a quadroon named "Madame John" after her lover who willed this house to her. There are no tours, but you can enjoy two exhibits, one on the history and legends of the house (including glimpses into the style and manner of Creole life), and another of art by self taught/primitive artists.

Musée Conti Wax Museum. 917 Conti St. ☎ **504/525-2605.** Fax 504/566-7636. www.get-waxed.com. Admission $6.25 adults, $5.50 seniors (over 62), $4.50 children 4–17, free for children under 4. Daily 10am–5:30pm. Closed Mardi Gras, Dec 25.

You might wonder about the advisability of a wax museum in a place as hot as New Orleans, but the Musée Conti is pretty neat—and downright spooky in spots. (And of course, when it is hot, this is a good place to cool off!) A large section is devoted to a sketch of Louisiana legends (Andrew Jackson, Napoléon, Jean Lafitte, Marie Laveau, Huey Long, a Mardi Gras Indian, Louis Armstrong, and Pete Fountain) and historical episodes. There's also a "Haunted Dungeon" in the true wax museum tradition, with monsters and scenes from well-known horror tales. It helps to think Vincent Price while you're here.

New Orleans Historic Voodoo Museum. 724 Dumaine St., at Bourbon. ☎ **504/523-7685.** Fax 504/523-8591. www.voodoomuseum.com. Admission $6.30 adults, $5.25 students and seniors. French Quarter tour $18, cemetery tour $14, Tour of the Undead $15. Daily 10am–8pm.

Some of the hard-core voodoo practitioners in town might scoff at the Voodoo Museum, and perhaps rightly so. It is largely designed for tourists, but is also probably the best opportunity for tourists to get acquainted with the history and culture of voodoo. Don't expect high-quality, comprehensive exhibits—the place is dark, dusty, and musty (once you pass through the gift store). There are occult objects from all over the globe, plus some articles that allegedly belonged to the legendary Marie Laveau. Unless someone on staff talks you through it—which they will, if you ask—you might come away with as much confusion as facts. Still, it's an adequate introduction—and who wouldn't want to bring home a voodoo doll from here? The people who run the museum are involved in voodoo, and there is generally a voodoo priestess on site, giving readings and making personal gris-gris bags. Again, voodoo for tourists, but for most tourists, probably the right amount. (Don't confuse this place with the Marie Laveau House of Voodoo on Bourbon Street.)

The museum also offers a **guided voodoo walking tour** of the French Quarter. It leaves the museum at 1pm weekdays and 10:30am on Sunday and visits Congo Square (now Beauregard Square). Another tour takes you to **St. Louis Cemetery No. 1** to visit Marie Laveau's reputed grave. The tours might be light on verifiable facts, but they are usually entertaining. (On the St. Louis tour, please don't scratch X's on the graves; no matter what you've heard, it is not a real voodoo practice, and is destroying fragile tombs.) The museum can arrange psychic readings and visits to voodoo rituals if you want to delve deeper into the subject.

New Orleans Pharmacy Museum. 514 Chartres St., at St. Louis. ☎ **504/565-8027.** Fax 504/565-8028. Admission $2 adults, $1 seniors and students, free for children under 12. Tues–Sun 10am–5pm.

Founded in 1950, the New Orleans Pharmacy Museum is just what the name implies. In 1823, the first licensed pharmacist in the United States, Louis J. Dufilho Jr., opened an apothecary shop here. The Creole-style town house doubled as his home, and he cultivated the herbs he needed for his medicines in the interior courtyard. Inside you'll find old apothecary bottles, voodoo potions, pill tile, and suppository molds, as well as the old glass cosmetics counter (pharmacists of the 1800s also manufactured makeup and perfumes).

Unfortunately, the old-timey atmosphere is assisted by itty-bitty information cards attached to the exhibits, with minimal facts listed in ancient typefaces or spidery handwriting. Too bad; as alternative medicine gains acceptance, it's fascinating to look back at a time when medicine was barely more than snake-oil potions. (You certainly come away with a new respect and gratitude for antibiotics.) A new exhibit that highlights "milestones in the history of pharmacy and medicine" is on the second floor, where one of the recent temporary shows was about the history of sexually transmitted disease and the dubious "cures" once available.

✪ **The Presbytère.** 751 Chartres St., Jackson Sq. ☎ **504/568-6968.** Admission $5 adults, $4 seniors and students, free for children under 13. Tues–Sun 9am–5pm.

The Presbytère was planned as housing for the clergy but was never used for that purpose. Currently, it's part of the Louisiana State Museum, which has announced plans to close the building in October, 1999, and reopen in January, 2000 entirely devoted to Mardi Gras.

While we will miss the witty and informative (if badly displayed) Baroness de Pontalba exhibit (and can only hope it will resurface in some other Louisiana State Museum property), the plans for this long-overdue exhibition promise something truly stunning and special. The new installation should focus on the origins and evolution of Carnival, including ancient religious festivals and Louisiana Mardi Gras' own 19th-century beginnings. The artifacts collected are staggering in variety and number. Computer and video technology will allow visitors to participate (in a virtual reality kind of way) in balls, parades, and other activities. Galleries will be devoted to themes; climb aboard a float in the Parade Gallery, or create a computer generated costume in the Masking Gallery. In short, learn about the rich history of Mardi Gras and why it's so much more than just a big debauched party. This could be quite a marvelous, if not definitive, addition to the Quarter. Time will tell.

Woldenberg Riverfront Park. ☎ 504/861-2537.

Made up of just under 20 acres of newly repaired green space, Woldenberg Riverfront Park stretches along the Mississippi from the elevated area called the Moonwalk (for former Mayor "Moon" Landrieu) at the old Governor Nicholls Street wharf to the Aquarium of the Americas at Canal Street (see above). This has historically been the city's promenade; now, it's an oasis of greenery in the heart of the city, with numerous works by popular local artists scattered throughout. The park includes a large lawn with a brick promenade leading to the Mississippi, and is home to hundreds of trees—oaks, magnolias, willows, and crape myrtles—and thousands of shrubs.

The Moonwalk has steps that allow you to get right down to Old Muddy—on foggy nights, you feel as if you are floating above the water. There are many benches from which to view the city's main industry—its busy port (second in the world only to Amsterdam in annual tonnage). To your right you'll see the Greater New Orleans Bridge and the World Trade Center of New Orleans (formerly the International Trade Mart) skyscraper, as well as the Toulouse Street wharf, departure point for excursion steamboats. The park is open daily, dawn to dusk.

2 Outside the French Quarter

UPTOWN & THE GARDEN DISTRICT

If you can see just one thing outside the French Quarter, make it the Garden District. It has no significant historic buildings or, with one exception (below), important museums. It's simply beautiful. In some ways, even more so than the Quarter, this is New Orleans. Authors as diverse as Truman Capote and Anne Rice have been enchanted by its spell. Gorgeous homes of superb design stand quietly amidst lush foliage, elegant, but ever-so-slightly (or more) decayed. You can see why this is the setting for so many novels; it's hard to imagine that anything real actually happens here.

But it does. Like the Quarter, this is a neighborhood, so please be courteous as you wander around.

TROLLING ST. JOHN'S BAYOU

St. John's Bayou is a body of water that originally extended from the outskirts of New Orleans to Lake Pontchartrain, and it's one of the most important reasons New Orleans is where it is today. Jean-Baptiste Le Moyne, Sieur de Bienville, who was commissioned to establish a settlement in Louisiana, chose the spot where New Orleans now sits because he recognized the strategic importance of "back-door" access to the Gulf of Mexico provided by the bayou's linkage to the lake.

The bayou is no longer navigable (even if it were, bridges were built too low to permit the passage of boats of any size), but residents still prize their waterfront sites, and rowboats and sailboats make use of the bayou's surface. It's one of the prettiest areas of New Orleans, full of the old houses tourists love to marvel at, but without the hustle, bustle and confusion of more high profile locations. A walk along the banks and through the nearby neighborhoods is one of our favorite things to do on a nice afternoon.

The simplest way to reach St. John's Bayou from the French Quarter is to drive straight out Esplanade Avenue about 20 blocks. Right before you reach the bayou, you'll pass **St. Louis Cemetery No. 3** (just past Leda Street). It's the final resting place of many prominent New Orleanians. Just past the cemetery, turn left onto Moss Street, which runs along the banks of St. John's Bayou. If you want to see an example of an 18th-century West Indies–style plantation house, stop at **the Pitot House,** 1440 Moss St. (see below).

To continue, drive along Wisner Boulevard, on the opposite bank of St. John's Bayou from Moss Street, and you'll pass some of New Orleans' grandest modern homes—a sharp contrast to those on Moss Street. If you want to go all the way to Lake Pontchartrain, here's a good route: Stay on Wisner to Robert E. Lee Boulevard, turn right, and drive to Elysian Fields Avenue, then turn left. Turn left onto the broad concrete highway, Lakeshore Drive. It runs for $5^1/_2$ miles along the lake, and in the summer the parkway alongside its seawall is usually swarming with swimmers and picnickers. On the other side are more luxurious, modern residences.

WHERE THE BODIES AREN'T BURIED

The cities of the dead are part of New Orleans' indelible landscape, along with Spanish moss and lacy iron balconies. Their ghostly and

New Orleans Attractions

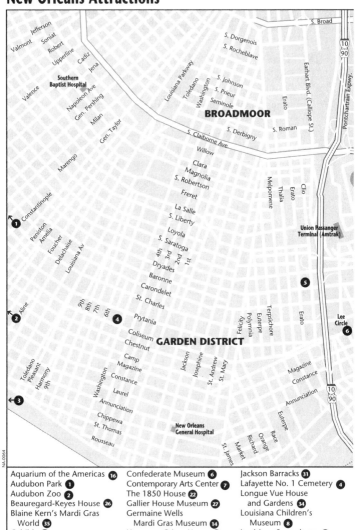

NA-0064

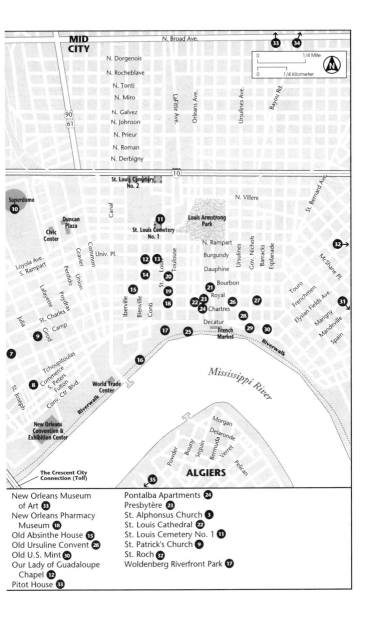

New Orleans Museum
of Art 33
New Orleans Pharmacy
Museum 18
Old Absinthe House 15
Old Ursuline Convent 28
Old U.S. Mint 30
Our Lady of Guadaloupe
Chapel 12
Pitot House 33

Pontalba Apartments 24
Presbytère 23
St. Alphonsus Church 3
St. Louis Cathedral 22
St. Louis Cemetery No. 1 11
St. Patrick's Church 9
St. Roch 32
Woldenberg Riverfront Park 17

inscrutable presence enthralls visitors, who are used to traditional methods of burial—in the ground or in mausoleums.

Why aboveground? Well, it rains in New Orleans. A lot. And then it floods. Soon after New Orleans was settled it became apparent that Uncle Etienne had an unpleasant habit of bobbing back to the surface (doubtless no longer looking his best). So in 1789, the city opened St. Louis No. 1, right outside the city walls, on what is now Rampart Street. The "condo crypt" look—the dead are placed in vaults that look like miniature buildings—was inspired to a certain extent by the famous Pere Lachaise cemetery in Paris.

These little houses of the dead, in addition to solving the problem of belowground burial, are even more functional. There are two types of crypts: the aforementioned "family vaults" and the "oven crypts"—so called because of their resemblance to bread ovens in a wall. A coffin is slid inside, and the combination of heat and humidity acts like a slow form of cremation. In a year or so, the occupant is reduced to bone. As the space is needed, the bones are pushed to the back, coffin pieces removed, and another coffin inserted. In the larger family vaults (made of whitewashed brick), there are a couple of shelves, and the same thing happens. As family members die, the bones are swept off the shelves into a pit below, and everyone eventually lies jumbled together.

You will be warned against going to the cemeteries alone, and urged to go with a scheduled tour group (see "Organized Tours," below). It is true that thanks to their location and layout, some cemeteries can be quite risky, making visitors prime pickings for muggers and so forth. Ironically, two of the most hazardous, St. Louis No. 1 and Lafayette No. 1, are often so full of tour groups that you could actually go there without one and be fairly safe. On the other hand, a good tour is fun and informative, so why not take the precaution?

Note: As of this writing, there is no regular tour of St. Louis No. 2, which is absolutely unsafe. Do not go there, even in a large group, without an official tour.

St. Louis No. 1. Basin St. between Conti and St. Louis sts.

The oldest extant cemetery (1789), and the most iconic. Here lie Marie Laveau, Bernard Marigny, and assorted other New Orleans characters. Louis the vampire from Anne Rice's *Vampire Chronicles* even has his (empty) tomb here. The acid-dropping scene from *Easy Rider* was shot here.

Sailing to Algiers

Algiers is considerably less high profile than the French Quarter or the Garden District, but it's every bit as much of a neighborhood, and very nearly as picturesque, if on a less grand scale. This is where you'll find some of the area's best-preserved examples of late-Victorian gingerbread houses and classic Creole cottages, set in a small neighborhood relatively unmoved by modernity. Exploring Algiers on foot is a wonderful way to spend an afternoon.

Taking the ferry to Algiers is a perfect way to get out onto the river—you can see the city's skyline and its significant geography without any hassle, and without having to pay a dime. (It's free for pedestrians.) The ferry runs every 15 to 20 minutes, and the heart of downtown New Orleans is only a stone's throw away, yet Algiers has never been fully assimilated into the city. It retains the feel of an undisturbed turn-of-the-century suburb.

Lafayette No. 1. 1427 Sixth St.

Right across the street from Commander's Palace restaurant, this is the lush uptown cemetery. Once in horrible condition, it's been beautifully restored. Anne Rice's Mayfair witches have their family tomb here.

HERE'S THE CHURCH & HERE'S THE STEEPLE . . .

Church and religion are not likely to be the first things that jump to mind in a city known for its debauchery. But New Orleans remains a very Catholic city. Don't forget that Mardi Gras is a pre-Lenten celebration. In fact, religion of one form or another directed much of the city's early history and molded its culture in countless ways.

St. Alphonsus Church. 2045 Constance St., at St. Andrews. ☎ **504/ 522-6748.**

The Irish built St. Alphonsus Church in 1855, because they refused to worship with their German-speaking neighbors. The gallery and columns may vaguely remind you of the St. Louis Cathedral in the French Quarter, though we find it more spooky and atmospheric. That's probably why portions of Anne Rice's "The Witching Hour" take place here. The church no longer holds Mass. Currently, the church operates an Arts and Cultural Center, which includes an Irish

Art museum. You can tour in the interior and the museum 2 days a week, Thursday and Saturday, from 10am to 2pm, with a self-guided audiotape (live tour guides must be arranged in advance.) For information, call the Friends of St. Alphonsus at ☎ **504/522-7420** or 504/482-0008.

St. Mary's Assumption. 2030 Assumption (at Josephine). ☎ **504/522-6748.**

Built in 1860 by the German Catholics, this is a more baroque and grand church than its Irish neighbor across the street, complete with dozens of life-size saints statues, and the beneficiary of a major restoration project. The hero of the yellow fever epidemic of 1867, Fr. Francis Xavier Seelos, is buried in the church. Credited with the working of many miracles, he will be beatified in 2000—and to say this is a big deal is to make an understatement. If you visit the church, you're likely to see letters of petition on his tomb. Still more "Witching Hour" action takes place here, including Rowan and Michael's wedding. The church is only open during Mass; call the office for times.

St. Patrick's Church. 724 Camp St., at Girod. ☎ **504/525-4413.**

The original St. Patrick's was a tiny wooden building founded to serve the spiritual needs of Irish Catholics. The present building, begun in 1838, was constructed around the old one. The distinguished architect James Gallier Sr., designed much of the interior, including the altar. It opened in 1840, proudly proclaiming itself as the "American" Catholics' answer to the St. Louis Cathedral in the French Quarter (where, according to the Americans, God spoke only in French).

St. Roch and the Campo Santo. 1725 St. Roch Ave., at N. Derbigny. ☎ **504/945-5961.**

St. Roch is the patron saint of plague victims; a local priest prayed to him to keep his flock safe during an epidemic in 1867. When everyone came through all right, the priest made good on his promise to build St. Roch a chapel. The Gothic result is fine enough, but what is best is the small room just off the altar, where successful supplicants to St. Roch leave gifts, usually in the form of plaster anatomical parts or medical supplies, to represent what the saint healed for them. The resulting collection of bizarre artifacts (everything from eyeballs and crutches to organs and false limbs) is either deeply moving or the greatest creepy spontaneous folk art installation you've ever seen. The chapel is not always open, so call first.

Church of St. John the Baptist. 1139 Dryades St., at US90. ☎ **504/525-1726.**

You may have noticed a large gilded dome prominently set in the New Orleans skyline (especially as you drive on the elevated expressway). That's the Church of St. John the Baptist, built by the Irish in 1871. Its most noteworthy features (besides the exceptional exterior brickwork) are the beautiful stained-glass windows and the Stations of the Cross and sacristy murals.

Our Lady of Guadeloupe Chapel—International Shrine of St. Jude. 411 N. Rampart St., at Conti. ☎ **504/525-1551.**

This is known as the "funeral chapel." It was erected (in 1826) conveniently near St. Louis Cemetery No. 1, specifically for funeral services, so as not to spread disease through the Quarter. Check out the statue of St. Expedite. He got his name, according to legend, when his crate arrived with no identification other than the word *expedite* stamped on the outside. Now he's the saint you pray to when you want things in a hurry. We are not making this up. He's just inside the door on the right—go say hi.

BUILDINGS WITH A HISTORY (& ONE WITH BULK)

Degas House. 2306 Esplanade Ave. ☎ **504/821-5009.** Admission and self-guided tour, free; guided tours, $5 donation requested. Daily 9am–6pm.

Legendary French impressionist Edgar Degas felt very tender toward New Orleans; his mother and grandmother were born here and he spent several months in 1872–73 visiting his brother at this house. It was a trip that resulted in a number of paintings, and this is the only residence or studio associated with Degas anywhere in the world that is open to the public.

Pitot House. 1440 Moss St., near Esplanade. ☎ **504/482-0312.** Fax 504/482-0312. Admission $5 adults, $4 seniors and students, $2 children under 12. Parties of 10 or more $3 each. Wed–Sat 10am–3pm. Last tour begins at 2pm.

The Pitot House is a typical West Indies–style plantation home, restored and furnished with early 19th-century Louisiana and American antiques. Dating from 1799, it originally stood where the nearby modern Catholic school is. In 1810 it became the home of James Pitot, the first mayor of incorporated New Orleans (he served 1804–05).

Jackson Barracks. 6400 St. Claude Ave. ☎ **504/271-6262,** ext. 242. Free admission. Museum hours Mon–Fri 7:30am–4pm.

On an extension of Rampart Street downriver from the French Quarter is this series of fine old brick buildings with white columns.

They were built in 1834–35 for troops who were stationed at the river forts. The barracks now serve as headquarters for the Louisiana National Guard, and there's an extensive military museum in the old powder magazine and in a new annex, which has a large collection of military items from every American war. Call before you go to confirm that the barracks and museum are open.

Superdome. 1500 block of Poydras St., near Rampart. ☎ **504/587-3808** for tour information. Admission $6 adults, $5 seniors, $4 children 5–10, free for children under 5. Guided tours daily 10am–4pm on the hour (except during events). Tours subject to change and cancellation.

Completed in 1975 (at a cost of around $180 million) the Superdome is a landmark civic structure. It's a 27-story windowless building with a seating capacity of 76,000 and a computerized climate-control system that uses more than 9,000 tons of equipment. It's one of the largest buildings in the world in diameter (680 feet), and its grounds cover some 13 acres. Inside, no posts obstruct the spectator's view of sporting events, be they football, baseball, or basketball, while movable partitions and seats allow the building to be configured for almost any event.

MUSEUMS & GALLERIES

Confederate Memorial Museum. 929 Camp St., at St. Joseph's. ☎ **504/523-4522.** Fax 504/523-8595. Admission $5 adults, $4 students and seniors, $2 children under 12. Mon–Sat 10am–4pm.

Not far from the French Quarter, the Confederate Museum was established in 1891 (giving it a claim to being the oldest surviving museum in Louisiana) and currently houses the second-largest collection of Confederate memorabilia in the country. The museum also has a series of detailed pictures tracing Louisiana's history from secession through Reconstruction.

✪ **Contemporary Arts Center.** 900 Camp St., at St. Joseph's. ☎ **504/523-1216.** Admission $5 adults, $3 seniors and students, free for members; free to all Thurs. Tickets $3–$25. Mon–Sat 10am–5pm, Sun 11am–5pm.

Redesigned in the early '90s to much critical applause, the Contemporary Arts Center is a main anchor of New Orleans' young arts district (once the city's old warehouse district, now home to a handful of leading local galleries). Over the past 2 decades, the center has consistently exhibited influential and groundbreaking work by regional, national, and international artists in various mediums. The CAC also presents theater, performance art, dance, and music concerts.

Gone With the Wind

Although most antebellum plantations have probably gone the way of the wind, you can still capture some of the Old South in the form of restored plantation homes. In just an hour jaunt from New Orleans, you can travel back over 100 years. Located on the same road (La. 18), you van visit both Laura Plantation and Oak Alley. The tours at Laura go into a lot more depth about Creole life, but the oaks at Oak Alley are a site to be seen—that is, if you didn't see them in *Interview with the Vampire.*

✪ **New Orleans Museum of Art.** 1 Collins Diboll Circle, at City Park and Esplanade. ☎ **504/488-2631.** Admission $6 adults, $5 seniors (over 64), $3 children 3–17; free to Louisiana residents Thurs 10am–noon. Tues–Sun 10am–5pm. Closed most major holidays.

Often called NOMA, this museum is located in an idyllic section of City Park. A $23 million expansion in 1994 tripled its size, and allowed NOMA to attract a variety of international and touring exhibits. The front portion of the museum is the original large, imposing neoclassical building; the rear portion is a striking contrast of curves and contemporary styles. It houses a 40,000-piece collection: pre-Columbian and Native American ethnographic art; 16th-through 20th-century European paintings, drawings, sculptures, and prints; early American art; Asian art; and one of the six largest decorative glass collections in the United States. Make sure you leave time to visit any temporary exhibits.

✪ **Blaine Kern's Mardi Gras World.** 223 Newton St., Algiers Point. ☎ **800/362-8213** or 504/361-7821. Fax 504/361-3164. www. mardigrasworld.com. Admission $9.50 adults, $6.50 seniors (over 62), $4 children 3–12. Daily 9:30am–4:30pm. Closed Mardi Gras, Easter, Thanksgiving, Dec 25. Cross the river on the Canal St. Ferry and take the free shuttle from the dock (it meets every ferry).

Few cities can boast a thriving float-making industry. New Orleans can, and no float-maker thrives more than Blaine Kern, who makes more than three-quarters of the floats used by the various krewes every Carnival season. Blaine Kern's Mardi Gras World offers tours of its collection of float sculptures and of its studios, where you can see floats being made year-round. The real attractions here, though, are the huge sculptures of cartoon and comic book characters, mythological figures, and imaginary creatures.

✪ **Laura: A Creole Plantation.** 2247 La. 18, Vacherie, LA 70090. ☎ **225/ 265-7690.** Fax 225/265-7690. www.lauraplantation.com. Admission $7 adults, $4 students and children, free for children under 6. Closed major holidays.

If you see only one plantation, make it this one. The hoopskirted tours found elsewhere are banished in favor of a comprehensive view of daily life on an 18th- and 19th-century plantation, a cultural history of Louisiana's Creole population, and a dramatic, entertaining, in-depth look at one extended Creole family.

This is a classic Creole house, simple on the outside, but with the real magic within. Unlike many other plantation homes, much is known about this house and the family that lived here, thanks to extensive records (more than 5,000 documents researched in France), particularly the detailed memoirs of Laura Local (for whom the plantation is named). On display are more than 375 original artifacts, making this the largest collection in the region of items belonging to one plantation family. They cover a 200-year period and include household items like clothes and jewelry. The property itself is a labor of love, as all the buildings are slowly being renovated (next up, the slave quarters).

Basic tours of the main building and the property last about 55 minutes and are organized around true (though spiced-up) stories from the history of the home and its residents. Special tours are available on subjects including Creole architecture, Creole women, children, slaves, and the "Americanization of Louisiana." The special tours last about 1½ hours and must be scheduled in advance. Every day, they offer tours in both English and French, and have handouts in several additional languages.

✪ **Oak Alley Plantation.** 3645 La. 18 (60 miles from New Orleans), Vacherie, LA 70090. ☎ **800/44-ALLEY** or 225/265-2151. Fax 225/265-2151. Admission $8 adults, $5 students, $3 children 6–12, free for children under 6. Mar–Oct daily 9am–5:30pm; Nov–Feb daily 9am–5pm. Closed Jan 1, Thanksgiving, Dec 25.

This is precisely what comes to mind when most people think "plantation." A splendid white house, its porch lined with giant columns, approached by a magnificent drive lined with stately oak trees—yep, it's all here. Consequently, this is the most famous (and probably most photographed) plantation house in Louisiana. (Parts of *Interview with a Vampire* and *Primary Colors* were shot here.) It's also the slickest operation, with a large parking lot, expensive lunch buffet (bring your own picnic), hoopskirted guides, and golf carts traversing the blacktopped lanes around the property.

The house was built in 1839 by Jacques Telesphore Roman III and named Bon Séjour—but if you walk out to the levee and look back at the quarter-mile avenue of 300-year-old live oaks, you'll see why steamboat passengers quickly dubbed it "Oak Alley." Roman was so enamored of the trees that he planned his house to have exactly as many columns—28 in all. The fluted Doric columns completely surround the Greek Revival house and support a broad second-story gallery. Little more is known about the families who lived here, consequently tours focus on more general plantation facts. But over the last few years, renovations have given the rooms and furnishings a facelift, returning the house to its 1830s roots. The furnishings are not original, but are strict to the time period and mostly correspond to the Romans' actual inventory.

Overnight accommodations are available in five turn-of-the-century Creole cottages (complete with sitting rooms, porches, and air-conditioning), with plans to add more in 2000. Rates are $85 to $115, and include breakfast but not a tour. The overpriced restaurant is open for breakfast and lunch daily from 9am to 3pm.

3 Parks & Gardens

PARKS

✪ **Audubon Park.** 6500 Magazine St., between Broadway and Exposition. ☎ **504/581-4629.**

Across from Loyola and Tulane universities, Audubon Park and the adjacent Audubon Zoo sprawl over 340 acres, extending from St. Charles Avenue all the way to the Mississippi River. This tract once belonged to New Orleans' founder Jean-Baptiste Le Moyne, and later was part of the Etienne de Boré plantation, where sugar was granulated for the first time in 1794. The city purchased it in 1871 and used much of the land for the World's Industrial and Cotton Centennial Exposition in 1884–85. Despite having the (then) largest building in the world as its main exhibition hall (33 acres under one roof), the exposition was such a financial disaster that everything except the Horticultural Hall had to be sold off—and that hall fell victim to a hurricane a little later. After that, serious work to make this into a park began.

Although John James Audubon, the country's best-known ornithologist, lived only briefly in New Orleans (in a cottage on Dauphine Street in the French Quarter), the city has honored him by naming both the park and the zoo after him.

Without question, the most utilized feature of the park is the 1³/₄-mile paved traffic-free road that loops around the lagoon and golf course. Between 2,000 and 3,000 joggers use the track each day, joined by cyclists, walkers, and in-line skaters. Along the track are 18 exercise stations; tennis courts and horseback riding facilities can be found elsewhere in the park. Check out the pavilion on the riverbank for one of the most pleasant views of the Mississippi you'll find. The Audubon Zoo is toward the back of the park, across Magazine Street.

Note: The park opens daily at 6am. Even though it officially closes at 10pm, it's not advisable to be there any time after dark.

✪ **City Park.** 1 Palm Dr. ☎ **504/482-4888.**

At the entrance you'll see a statue of Gen. P. G. T. Beauregard, whose order to fire on Fort Sumter opened the Civil War and whom New Orleanians fondly call "the Great Creole." The extensive, beautifully landscaped grounds hold botanical gardens and a conservatory, four golf courses, picnic areas, a restaurant, lagoons for boating and fishing, tennis courts, horses for hire and lovely trails to ride them on, a bandstand, two miniature trains, and Children's Storyland, an amusement area with a carousel ride for children (see "Especially for Kids," below). At Christmastime, the mighty oaks, already dripping with Spanish moss, are strung with lights—quite a magical sight—and during Halloween, there is a fabulous haunted house. You'll also find the New Orleans Museum of Art at Collins Diboll Circle, on Lelong Avenue, in a building that is itself a work of art (see "Museums & Galleries," above). The park's main office is in the casino building. The park is open daily 6am to 7pm.

GARDENS

Longue Vue House & Gardens. 7 Bamboo Rd., near Metairie. ☎ **504/488-5488.** Admission $7 adults, $6 seniors, $3 children and students. Mon–Sat 10am–4:30pm, Sun 1–5pm. Closed Jan 1, Mardi Gras, July 4, Labor Day, Thanksgiving, Dec 25.

The Longue Vue mansion is a unique expression of Greek Revival architecture, set on an 8-acre estate. It was constructed from 1939 to 1942 for Edgar Stern, who had interests in cotton, minerals, timber, and real estate, and was also a noted philanthropist and a founder (with his son) of local television station WDSU-TV. Styled in the manner of an English country house, their mansion was designed to foster a close rapport between indoors and outdoors, with vistas of formal terraces and pastoral woods. Some parts of the

Mid City Attractions

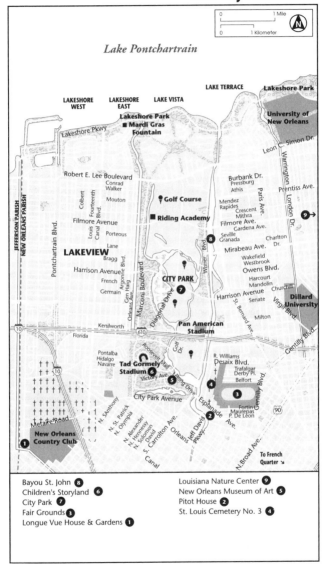

Lake Pontchartrain

Bayou St. John ⑧
Children's Storyland ⑥
City Park ⑦
Fair Grounds ⑧
Longue Vue House & Gardens ①

Louisiana Nature Center ⑨
New Orleans Museum of Art ⑤
Pitot House ②
St. Louis Cemetery No. 3 ④

enchanting gardens were inspired by those of Generalife, the former summer house of the sultans in Granada, Spain.

Louisiana Nature Center (in Joe Brown Memorial Park). Nature Center Dr., New Orleans East. ☎ **504/246-5672** or 504/246-9381. www. audoboninstitute.org. Admission $4.75 adults, $3.75 seniors, $2.50 children. Tues–Fri 9am–5pm, Sat 10am–5pm, Sun noon–5pm. Take I-10 to Exit 244; pass Plaza Shopping Center and turn left onto Nature Center Dr.

Part of the Audubon Institute, Joe Brown Park is an 86-acre tract of Louisiana forest where guided walks are given daily (except Monday). A nature film is shown on weekdays, and weekends offer additional activities (canoeing, bird watching, arts and crafts workshops, and others). Three miles of trails are available for public use. There is a wheelchair-accessible raised wooden walkway for shorter excursions. The Louisiana Nature Center offers changing exhibits and hands-on activities. It has a planetarium where there are shows on Saturday and Sunday, and on Friday and Saturday nights there are laser rock shows. Call ☎ 504/246-STAR for the current planetarium schedule.

A DAY AT THE ZOO

✪ **Audubon Zoo.** 6500 Magazine St. ☎ **504/581-4629.** Admission $8.75 adults, $4.75 seniors (over 64) and $4.50 children 2–12. Daily 9:30am–5pm; 9:30am–6pm weekends in the summer. Last ticket sold 1 hour before closing. Closed holidays.

It's been more than 20 years since the Audubon Zoo underwent a total renovation that turned it from one of the worst zoos in the country into one of the best. Here, in a setting of subtropical plants, waterfalls, and lagoons, some 1,800 animals (including rare and endangered species) live in natural habitats rather than cages. Don't miss the replica of a Louisiana swamp or the new "Butterflies in Flight" exhibit, where more than 1,000 butterflies live among lush, colorful vegetation. A memorable way to visit the zoo is to arrive on the sternwheeler *John James Audubon* (see "Organized Tours," below) and depart on the St. Charles Avenue streetcar. You can reach the streetcar by walking through Audubon Park or by taking the free shuttle bus.

4 Especially for Kids

New Orleans is one of those destinations that may be more fun *sans enfants*. Don't get us wrong—there are plenty of unusual things to do during daylight hours that will wear out everyone under 12 or over 40, but any adult confined to his or her hotel room past 9pm has entirely missed the point of vacationing here. But until they're old enough to go clubbing with Mom and Dad, you can entertain them with a combination of conventional and unconventional, only-in-New-Orleans activities. The Aquarium of the Americas, the Zoo, the Musee Conti Wax Museum, a walk through the French Quarter with a stop for beignets, a ride on a streetcar or Mississippi ferry—all these should keep their good times rollin'.

The following destinations are particularly well-suited for younger children.

Children's Storyland. City Park at Victory Ave. ☎ **504/483-9381.** Admission $2 adults and children 2 and up, free for children under 2. Wed–Fri 10am–12:30pm, Sat–Sun 10am–4:30pm. Closed weekdays Jan–Feb and Dec.

The under-8 set will be delighted with this playground (rated one of the 10 best in the country by *Child* magazine), where well-known children's stories and rhymes have inspired the decor. Kids and adults will enjoy the carousel, Ferris wheel, bumper cars, and other rides at the **Carousel Gardens,** also in City Park. It's open weekends only, 11am to 4:30pm. Admission is $1 for anyone over 2; $6 buys unlimited rides. If you happen to arrive in New Orleans during December, be sure to take a carriage ride through City Park, when thousands of lights turn the landscape and trees into fairy-tale scenery.

Louisiana Children's Museum. 420 Julia St., at Tchoupitoulis. ☎ **504/523-1357.** Admission $5. Sept–May Tues–Sat 9:30am–4:30pm, Sun noon–4:30pm; June–Aug Mon 9:30am–4:30pm.

This popular two-story interactive museum is really a playground in disguise that will keep kids occupied for a good couple of hours. Along with changing exhibits, the museum offers an art shop with regularly scheduled projects, a minigrocery store, a chance to be a "star anchor" at a simulated television studio, and lots of activities exploring music, fitness, water, and life itself. If you belong to your local science museum, check your membership card for reciprocal entry privileges.

5 Organized Tours

Though this book should give you plenty of information to help you guide yourself around the city and gain some understanding of it, another option is to hook up with a tour. A guided excursion can offer something a little more in-depth or, if you prefer, specific: Various tours cater to just about every interest, from African American history to vampires and ghosts.

IN THE FRENCH QUARTER

✪ **Historic New Orleans Walking Tours** (☎ 504/947-2120) is the place to go for authenticity. Tour guides are carefully chosen for their combination of knowledge and entertaining manner. They offer a "French Quarter Mystique" walking tour, a distinctive gumbo of legend and fact." Now that the National Park Service has stopped doing tours, this is probably the best, straightforward, nonspecialized walking tour of the Quarter. Daily, 10:30am. Leaves from C. C.'s Coffee Shop at 528 Peter St. on Jackson Square, $12 adults/$10 students and seniors. They also offer a Voodoo tour (see "Mystical & Mysterious Tours," later in this chapter).

The nonprofit volunteer group **Friends of the Cabildo** (☎ 504/523-3939) offers an excellent walking tour. The organization supports the Cabildo, the building on Chartres Street where the Louisiana Purchase was signed. The tour furnishes guides for a 2-hour exploration that provides a good overview of the area. It leaves from in front of the Museum Store, 523 St. Ann St. Your guide will point out and provide background on the exteriors of most of the Quarter's historic buildings and on the interiors of selected Louisiana State Museum buildings. The requested donation is $10 per adult, $8 for seniors (over 65) and children 13 to 20; it's free for children under 13. Tours leave Tuesday through Sunday at 10am and 1:30pm and Monday at 1:30pm, except holidays. No reservations are necessary—just show up, donation in hand. The Friends also offer seasonal tours—like the terrific one offered at Halloween, of local courtyards otherwise not open to the public, where guides dressed as the ghosts of local historical figures tell their tales.

Stop by the **Jean Lafitte National Park and Preserve's Folklife and Visitor Center,** 419 Decatur St. (☎ 504/589-2636), for details on its excellent free walking tour conducted by National Park Service rangers. The History of New Orleans tour covers about a mile in the French Quarter and brings to life New Orleans' history and the ethnic roots of the city's unique cultural mix. No reservations are required for this tour but only 30 people are taken in a group. The tour starts at 10:30am daily (except for Mardi Gras), so as the office opens at 9am, it's strongly suggested you get there then to ensure you will get a ticket.

✪ **The Bienville Foundation,** run by Robert Batson (☎ 504/945-6789), offers a number of high-quality specialty tours created by expert scholars and researchers about various aspects of New

Orleans' multifaceted, dynamic, and rich culture. For variety and professionalism, this organization can't be beat. The slate of tours changes seasonally and has included a Scandal Tour, a highly popular and recommended Gay Heritage Tour, a Women's History tour, Black History, Writers in New Orleans, Jazz History, and Architecture. Tours last roughly two hours, and generally cost $20 per person. Times and departure locations also change seasonally so call to find out what's happening when.

Kenneth Holdrich, a professor of American literature at the University of New Orleans, runs ✪ **Heritage Literary Tours,** 732 Frenchmen St. (☎ **504/949-9805**). Since 1974, Holdrich has conducted literary walking tours of the French Quarter, and unlike some tour operators, he really knows his stuff. Aside from his considerable academic credentials, he knew both Tennessee Williams and the mother of John Kennedy Toole. In addition to a general tour, you can take the Williams-specific tour (T. W. covered a lot of ground in the place he called his "spiritual home"). Some tours, arranged in advance, can be designed around a specific author. The narratives are full of facts both literary and historical, loaded with anecdotes, and often downright humorous. Tours ($20 for adults, $10 for student group rate) are "scheduled for your convenience." Holdrich also does a regularly scheduled weekly tour for the Bienville Foundation, above.

If you want something a tab naughtier, you—and by "you," we mean adults—you can try **Red Light Tours' "Historic Storyville Tour"** (☎ **504/782-1170**), covering the unique history of that much-missed district, plus burlesque history of Bourbon Street, including detailing some of the famous acts of certain notorious dancing girls of the past. Tours depart Thursday to Monday, 11:30am and 2:30pm, from A Gallery Named Desire, 315 Decatur St., $20 per person (includes admission into the "gentlemen's club" of your choice).

✪ **Le Monde Creole** ☎ **504/568-1801**) offers a unique tour that uses the dramatic lives of one classic Creole family as a microcosm of the Creole world of the 19th century. You can learn about Creole city life, and the extraordinary story of Laura's family, off the plantation and in the Vieux Carre, while viewing French Quarter courtyards associated with the family. Guides are some of the best in the city, and this is probably the only operation that also offers tours in French. Tours leave from 624 Royal St., Tuesday through Saturday at 10:30am and 2:30pm. Reservations are required.

BEYOND THE FRENCH QUARTER

Author Robert Florence (who has written two excellent books about
New Orleans cemeteries) loves his work, and his ✪ **Historic New
Orleans Walking Tours** (☎ **504/947-2120**) are full of meticulously researched facts and more than a few good stories. A very
thorough tour of the Garden District and Lafayette Cemetery (a section of town not many of the other companies go into) leaves daily
at 11am and 1:45pm from the Garden District Book Shop (in the
Rink, corner of Washington Avenue and Prytania Street). Rates are
$14, students and seniors $12, free for children under 12.

    Tours by Isabelle (☎ **504/391-3544**), conducts a 3-hour, 45-
mile city tour for small groups in an air-conditioned minibus. The
tour covers the French Quarter, the cemeteries, St. John's Bayou,
City Park and the lakefront, the universities, St. Charles Avenue, the
Garden District, and the Superdome. The fare is $33, and departure
times are 9am and 1:30pm. Make reservations as far in advance as
possible. For $37 you can join Isabelle's afternoon Combo Tour,
which begins at 1pm and adds Longue Vue Gardens to all of the
above.

    Gray Line, 2 Canal St., Suite 1300 (☎ **800/535-7786** or 504/
587-0861), offers tours of the entire city, including the French
Quarter, in comfortable motor coaches. But take my word for it:
The Quarter demands a more in-depth examination than a view
from a bus window will provide. Take one of these excellent (and
very informative) tours only after you've explored the Quarter in
detail, or as a prelude to doing so.

    Gray Line also offers a tour that includes a 2-hour cruise on the
steamboat _Natchez._ You can have lunch on board (not included in
the tour price) as you take in the sights and sounds of the world's
second-busiest port. Gray Line picks up at various hotels throughout the city. You can also take the **River Road Plantation Tour,**
which departs daily at 9am, or the **Oak Alley Tour,** which leaves
at 1pm daily. The plantation tours operate on a different schedule
during December and January, so call for details.

    Gray Line has also added walking tours to its offerings, includ-
ing one of the Garden District and one of the French Quarter. Call
for times and departure points.

    Good Old Days (☎ **504/523-0804**), offers a 3-hour van tour
of the city, taking in sights in the Quarter, the Garden District, and
along Esplanade Avenue; visiting a cemetery; stopping in City Park;
and driving along the shore of Lake Pontchartrain. The tours begin

at 9am and 2pm daily; tickets are $30. The company also offers a plantation tour and carriage tours.

SWAMP TOURS

In addition to the tour providers listed below, Jean Lafitte and Gray Line (see above) both offer swamp tours. Swamp tours can be a hoot, particularly if you get a guide who calls alligators to your boat for a little snack of chicken (please keep your hands inside the boat—they tend to look a lot like chicken to a gator). On all of the following tours you're likely to see alligators, bald eagles, waterfowl, egrets, owls, herons, ospreys, feral hogs, otters, beavers, frogs, turtles, minks, raccoons, black bears, deer, and nutria.

Half Pint's Swamp Adventures (☎ **318/280-5976** or 318/288-1544) offers private guided tours of the "beauty, serenity, and exotic wildlife" of the Atchafalaya Basin, the nation's largest swamp. Half Pint is more folk hero than man, and his tours come highly recommended.

Lil' Cajun Swamp Tours (☎ **800/725-3213** or 504/689-3213) offers a good tour of Lafitte's bayous. Captain Cyrus Blanchard, "a Cajun French–speaking gentleman," knows the bayous like the back of his hand. The tour lasts 2 hours and costs about $16 for adults, $14 for seniors, and $12 for children 6 to 12 if you drive yourself to the boat launch. With transportation from New Orleans, the cost is $30 for adults, $15 for children. (Note that the boat used on the Lil' Cajun Swamp Tours is much larger than the boat used on many of the other tours—it seats up to 67 people, and can be noisier and more crowded than you might like.)

Dr. Wagner's Honey Island Swamp Tours (☎ **504/641-1769** or 504/242-5877), take you by boat into the interior of Honey Island Swamp's "most beautiful and pristine areas" to view wildlife with native professional naturalist guides. Dr. Wagner, the primary tour guide, is a trained wetland ecologist, and provides a solid educational experience to go with the purer swamp excitement. Tours last approximately 2 hours. Prices are $20 for adults, $10 for children under 12, if you drive to the launch site yourself; the rate is $40 if you want a hotel pickup in New Orleans.

Gator Swamp Tours (☎ **800/875-4287** or 504/484-6100), also takes visitors on a ride through Honey Island Swamp. Prices are $20 for adults, $10 for children under 12. The company offers a short nature walk in addition to boat tours. Like the other tour groups, Gator Swamp Tours offers hotel pickups for a fee. Tour operators

Karen and Danny have also converted an old river tugboat into a bed-and-breakfast, and are preparing an alligator exhibit as well.

MYSTICAL & MYSTERIOUS TOURS

An increased interest in the supernatural, ghostly side of New Orleans—let's go right ahead and blame Anne Rice—has meant an increased number of tours catering to the vampire set. Go for the entertainment value, not for the education (with some exceptions— see below).

Magic Walking Tours, 1015 Iberville St. (☎ **504/588-9693**), created by Richard Rochester, was apparently the first to up the ante on the evening tours, offering a bit of theatrical spectacle along with ghost stories. When others copied the concept, Rochester toned down the gimmicks. The guides are generally good, but Richard's the best—he knows how to spin a yarn, and his history of the town is marvelous to listen to. Several guided walking tours are offered daily: St. Louis Cemetery No. 1 (which is probably the only voodoo-free cemetery tour out there), the French Quarter, the Garden District, the Voodoo Tour, and the Vampire and Ghost-Hunt Walking Tour. Reservations are not necessary, but call ahead for tour schedules. Meeting places vary according to the tour. Tours cost $13, $10 students and seniors, and are free for children under 12.

Haunted History Tours, 97 Fontainebleau Dr. (☎ **888/6-GHOSTS** or 504/861-2727), is the Magic Walking Tours' big rival, and the place to go if you want theatrics along with facts (and we use the term very loosely). Expect fake snakes and blood, costumes, and gizmos. The Voodoo/Cemetery Tour explores St. Louis Cemetery No. 1 and provides a kind of voodoo cultural history; it departs Monday through Saturday at 10am and 1:15pm, Sunday at 10am only, and departs from Reverend Zombie's Voodoo Shop at 723 St. Peter St. The Haunted History Tour wanders the Quarter in search of its ghost stories and legends; it begins daily at 2 and 8pm departs from Reverend Zombie's Voodoo Shop at 723 St. Peter St. The nocturnal vampire tour of the Quarter starts at 8:30pm nightly and departs from the front steps of the St. Louis Cathedral. All three tours last 2 hours and cost $15 for adults and $7 for children under 13. The Garden District Tour Departs 10:30am and 1:30pm daily from the lobby of the Ramada Hotel at 2203 St. Charles Ave.

Historic New Orleans Walking Tours (☎ **504/947-2120**), best known for their extremely accurate walking tours of the Quarter and the Garden District, also offers a Cemetery and Voodoo Tour. The trip goes through St. Louis Cemetery No. 1, Congo Square, and an active voodoo temple. It leaves Monday through Saturday at 10am and 1pm, Sunday at 10am only, from the courtyard at 334-B Royal St. Rates are $15, students and seniors $13, free for children under 12.

BOAT TOURS

For those interested in doing the Mark Twain thing, a number of operators offer riverboat cruises. Docks are at the foot of Toulouse and Canal streets, and there's ample parking. Call for reservations, which are required for all these tours, and to confirm prices and schedules.

The steamboat *Natchez,* 2 Canal St., Suite 1300 (☎ **800/ 233-BOAT** or 504/586-8777), a marvelous three-deck sternwheeler docked at the wharf behind the Jackson Brewery, offers two 2-hour daytime cruises daily. The narration is by professional guides, and there are cocktail bars, live jazz, an optional Creole buffet, and a gift shop. Daytime fares are $14.75 for adults and $7.25 for children; evening cruises (not including dinner) are $22.50 for adults, $11.25 for children. Children under 3 ride free.

Aboard the sternwheeler *John James Audubon,* 2 Canal St., Suite 1300 (☎ **800/233-BOAT** or 504/586-8777), passengers travel the Mississippi, tour the busy port, and dock to visit the Audubon Zoo and the Aquarium of the Americas. There are four trips daily, departing from the Riverwalk in front of the Aquarium at 10am, noon, 2pm, and 4pm. Return trips from the zoo leave at 11am, 1pm, 3pm, and 5pm. Tickets for one-way or round-trips can be purchased with or without aquarium and zoo admission. Combination tickets are available that will save you several dollars.

The paddle wheeler *Creole Queen,* Riverwalk Dock (☎ **800/ 445-4109** or 504/524-0814), departs from the Poydras St. Wharf adjacent to the Riverwalk, at 10:30am and 2pm for 3-hour narrated excursions to the port and to the historic site of the Battle of New Orleans. There is also a 7pm jazz dinner cruise. The ship has a covered promenade deck, and its inner lounges are air-conditioned and heated. Buffet and cocktail service are available on all cruises. Daytime fares are $14 for adults, $7 for children; the nighttime jazz cruise is $42 for adults, $21 for children. Children under 3 ride free.

CARRIAGE TOURS

Corny it may be, but there is a sheepish romantic lure to the old mule-drawn carriages that pick up passengers at Jackson Square and take them for day and nighttime tours of the Quarter. The mules are decked out with ribbons, flowers, or even hats, and the drivers seem to be in a fierce competition to win the "most unusual city story" award. Once again, the "facts" presented are probably dubious, but should be most entertaining. Carriages wait at the Decatur Street end of Jackson Square from 9am to midnight in good weather; the charge is $8 per adult and $5 for children under 12.

Private horse-and-carriage tours offered by **Good Old Days Buggies** (☎ **504/523-0804**) include hotel or restaurant pickup and cost significantly more (between $30 and $115, depending on route and length of ride).

ANTIQUING TOURS

Antiquing in New Orleans can be an overwhelming experience, especially if you've never been to the city before, and even *more* especially if you have your heart set on something in particular. For that, you might need a little expert help, and that's why Macon Riddle founded **Let's Go Antiquing!**, 1412 Fourth St. (☎ **504/899-3027**), in the mid-1980s. She'll organize and customize antique shopping tours to fit your needs. Hotel pickup is included, and she will even make lunch reservations for you. If you find something and need to ship it home, she'll take care of that, too. There's no doubt in my mind that Macon Riddle is the best in the business.

7

Shopping

Shopping in New Orleans is a highly evolved leisure activity, with a shop for every strategy and a fix for every shopaholic—and every budget. Don't assume those endless T-shirt shops on Bourbon, or even the costly antique stores on Royal, are all New Orleans has to offer. The range is as good as it gets—many a clever person has come to New Orleans just to open up a quaint boutique filled with strange items gathered from all parts of the globe, or produced by local, somewhat twisted, folk artists.

1 The Shopping Scene

CANAL PLACE At the foot of Canal Street (365 Canal St.), where it reaches the Mississippi River, this shopping center holds more than 50 shops, many of them branches of some of this country's most elegant retailers. The three-tiered mall has polished marble floors, a landscaped atrium, fountains, and pools. Stores in this sophisticated setting include Brooks Brothers, Bally of Switzerland, Saks Fifth Avenue, Gucci, Williams-Sonoma, and Jaeger. Open Monday to Wednesday 10am to 6pm, Thursday 10am to 8pm, Friday and Saturday 10am to 7pm, and Sunday noon to 6pm.

THE FRENCH MARKET Shops within the Market begin on Decatur Street across from Jackson Square; offerings include candy, cookware, fashion, crafts, toys, New Orleans memorabilia, and candles. It's open 10am to 6pm (and the Farmer's Market Café du Monde is open 24 hours). Quite honestly, there is a lot of junk, but there are some good buys mixed in, and it's always fun to stroll through—and grab a nibble.

JACKSON BREWERY Just across from Jackson Square at 600–620 Decatur St., the old brewery building has been transformed into a jumble of shops, cafes, delicatessens, restaurants, and entertainment. The wares at the 125 shops, restaurants, and cafes within its walls include fashion, gourmet and Cajun-Creole foodstuffs, toys, hats, crafts, pipes, posters, and souvenirs. The latest addition to this mall is a branch of the theme restaurant Planet Hollywood. Keep in mind that many shops in the Brewery close at 5:30 or 6pm, before the Brewery itself. Open Sunday to Thursday 10am to 9pm, Friday and Saturday 10am to 10pm.

JULIA STREET From Camp Street down to the river on Julia Street, you'll find many of the city's best contemporary art galleries. Of course, some of the works are a bit pricey, but there are good deals to be had if you're collecting, and fine art to be seen if you're not. You'll find many of them listed below.

MAGAZINE STREET This is the Garden Disrict's premier shopping street. More than 140 shops (some of which are listed below), line the street in 19th-century brick storefronts and quaint cottagelike buildings. Among the offerings are antiques, art galleries, boutiques, crafts, and dolls. The greatest concentration of stores is between Felicity and Washington streets, but if you're so inclined, you could shop your way from here all the way to Audubon Park.

NEW ORLEANS CENTRE New Orleans' newest shopping center, at 1400 Poydras St., features a glass atrium and includes upscale stores like Lord & Taylor and Macy's. There are three levels of specialty shops and restaurants. Open Monday to Saturday 10am to 8pm and Sunday noon to 6pm.

RIVERBEND The Riverbend district is in the Carrollton area. To reach it, ride the St. Charles Avenue streetcar to stop 44, then walk down Maple Street 1 block to Dublin Park, the site of an old public market once lined with open stalls. Nowadays, renovated shops inhabit the old general store, a produce warehouse made of barge board, and the town surveyor's raised-cottage home. Among the outstanding shops are Yvonne LaFleur, whose romantic fashions have appeared on TV and movie screens, and the Cache Pot, with a concentration of unusual, high-quality gifts.

RIVERWALK MARKETPLACE This popular shopping development at 1 Poydras St. is an exciting covered mall that runs right along the river from Poydras Street to the Convention Center. If you have to go to a mall, it's a mighty pretty one (and a decent place to get out of the rain). In December 1996, the market made big news around the world when it was struck by a grain freighter descending the river; a number of shops were damaged, but there were no fatalities and everything was back in place shortly afterward. Among the 140 specialty shops, you'll find Eddie Bauer, the Limited, the Sharper Image, and Banana Republic, plus several places to eat and periodic free entertainment. Open Monday to Thursday 10am to

9pm, Friday and Saturday 10am to 10pm, and Sunday 12:30 to 5:30pm.

2 Shopping A to Z

ANTIQUES

Audubon Antiques. 2025 Magazine St. ☎ **504/581-5704.** Mon–Sat 10:30am–5pm, Sun 11am–5pm.

Audubon has everything from collectible curios to authentic antique treasures at reasonable prices. There are two floors of goods, so be prepared to lose yourself.

Boyer Antiques–Dolls & Buttons. 241 Chartres St. ☎ **504/522-4513.** Mon–Sat 11am–5pm.

In addition to an assortment of antiques, you'll find an enchanting collection of old dolls, doll houses and furniture, and toys. Most date from the 19th and early 20th centuries.

✪ **Bush Antiques and Beds Au Beau Reve.** 2109–2111 Magazine St. ☎ **504/581-3518.** Mon–Sat 10am–5pm.

This wonderful treasure trove features impressive European religious art and objects and a beautiful array of beds. An extra treat is the collection of folk art on the rear patio.

Dixon & Dixon of Royal. 237 Royal St. ☎ **800/848-5148** or 504/524-0282. Mon–Sat 9am–5:30pm, Sun 10am–5pm.

Dixon & Dixon features 18th- and 19th-century European fine art and antiques, jewelry, grandfather clocks, and Oriental rugs. The collection of tall-case clocks is one of the largest in the country; the individual clocks are awe-inspiring.

Jack Sutton Antiques. 315 Royal St. ☎ **504/522-0555.** Daily 10am–5pm.

There are a number of Suttons around New Orleans, mostly on Royal. This one, our favorite, specializes in jewelry and objects. The selection of estate jewelry is often better than that at other antique stores—the author's engagement ring came from here—but thanks to the ebb and flow of the estate business, you can never be sure what may be offered.

✪ **Lucullus.** 610 Chartres St. ☎ **504/528-9620.** Mon–Sat 9:30am–5pm.

An unusual shop, Lucullus has a wonderful collection of culinary antiques as well as 17th-, 18th-, and 19th-century furnishings to "complement the grand pursuits of cooking, dining, and imbibing." They have recently opened a second shop at 3932 Magazine St.

Magazine Arcade Antiques. 3017 Magazine St. ☎ **504/895-5451.** Mon and Wed–Sat 10am–5pm.

This large, fascinating shop holds an exceptional collection of 18th- and 19th-century European, Asian, and American furnishings as well as music boxes, dollhouse miniatures, European and Oriental porcelain, cloisonné, lacquer, cameos, opera glasses, old medical equipment, windup phonographs, antique toys, and scores of other items. Try to allow plenty of time to browse through it all.

Manheim Galleries. 403–409 Royal St. ☎ **504/568-1901.** Mon–Sat 9am–5pm.

At Manheim Galleries you'll find an enormous collection of continental, English, and Oriental furnishings sharing space with porcelains, jade, silver, and fine paintings. Manheim Galleries is also the agent for Boehm Birds.

✪ **Rothschild's Antiques.** 241 and 321 Royal St. ☎ **504/523-5816** or 504/523-2281. Mon–Sat 9:30am–5:30pm; Sun by appointment.

Rothschild's is a fourth-generation furniture merchandiser. Some of the most interesting things you'll find here are antique and custommade jewelry (the store is also a full-service jeweler). There's a fine selection of antique silver, marble mantels, porcelains, and English and French furnishings.

ART GALLERIES

With one major exception, galleries in New Orleans follow the landscape of antique shops: Royal and Magazine streets. Since the opening of the Contemporary Arts Center, galleries also have kept popping up around Julia Street and the warehouse district. Some are listed below, and there are others. All are strong contemporary fine art galleries, but it can be hard to tell them apart. The brochure "Arts in the Warehouse District" (call for it at ☎ **504/394-1515**) lists all of the galleries on Julia Street and some of the surrounding streets. If you're contemplating a gallery-hopping jaunt, start at Julia Street.

Ariodante. 535 Julia St. ☎ **504/524-3233.** Mon–Sat 11am–5pm. Closed Mon during daylight saving time.

A contemporary craft gallery, Ariodante features hand-crafted furniture, glass, ceramics, jewelry, and decorative accessories by nationally acclaimed artists. Rotating shows offer a detailed look at works by various artists.

✪ **Arthur Roger Gallery.** 432 Julia St. ☎ **504/522-1999.** www.artroger.com. Mon–Sat 10am–5pm.

Arthur Roger sets the pace for the city's fine art galleries. Since opening in New Orleans 20 years ago, Roger has played a major role in developing the art community and in tying it to the art world in New York. Time and again he has taken chances, scheduling shows that range from strongly regional work to the far-flung. The gallery represents many artists, including Francis Pavy (who did the 1997 Jazz Fest poster), Ida Kohlmeyer, Douglas Bourgeois, Ersy Schwartz, Paul Lucas, Clyde Connell, Willie Birch, Gene Koss, and George Dureau.

Bergen Galleries. 730 Royal St. ☎ **800/621-6179** or 504/523-7882. www.bergengalleries.com. Sun–Thurs 9am–9pm, Fri–Sat 9am–10pm.

Bergen Galleries has the city's largest selection of posters and limited-edition graphics, on such subjects as Mardi Gras, jazz, and the city itself, and by such artists as Erté, Icart, Nagel, Maimon, and Tarkay. Bergen also features a large collection of works by sought-after African American artists.

Berta's and Mina's Antiquities. 4138 Magazine St. ☎ **504/895-6201.** Mon–Sat 10am–6pm, Sun 11am–6pm.

In years past, Antiquities was just another place that bought and sold antiques and secondhand furniture and art. That all ended on the day in 1993 that Nilo Lanzas (Berta's husband and Mina's dad) began painting. Now you can barely see the furniture in the shop for all the new art. Dubbed "folk art" or "outsider art," Lanzas' works are colorful scenes from life in New Orleans or his native Latin America, stories out of the Bible, or images sprung from his imagination. His paintings are on wood with titles or commentaries painted on the frames; he also makes some tin sculptures and wood carvings. If you drop in, don't be surprised to find Lanzas quietly painting away near the counter—he paints 10 to 12 hours a day.

Bryant Galleries. 316 Royal St. ☎ **800/844-1994** or 504/525-5584. Sun–Thurs 10am–5:30pm, Fri–Sat 10am–9pm.

This gallery represents renowned artists Ed Dwight, Fritzner Lamour, and Leonardo Nierman, and other American, European, and Haitian artists. The varied work on display here may include jazz bronzes, glasswork, and graphics.

✪ **Casey Willems Pottery.** 3919 Magazine St. ☎ **504/899-1174.** Mon–Sat 10am–5pm.

Watch Casey Willems create functional art on his pottery wheel as you browse his gallery. You'll find bowls, lamps, pitchers, vases, and teapots, all created in the shop.

✪ **The Davis Galleries.** 3964 Magazine St. ☎ **504/897-0780.** Tues–Sat 10am–5pm.

One of two world-class galleries in New Orleans (the other being A Galley for Fine Photography), this may be the best place in the world for Central and West African traditional art. Works on display might include sculpture, costuming, basketry, textiles, weapons, and jewelry.

Diane Genre Oriental Art and Antiques. 431 Royal St. ☎ **504/595-8945.** www.dianegenreorientalart.com. By appointment only.

If all of the 18th- and 19th-century European antiques in the stores along Royal are starting to look the same, it's time to step into Diane Genre's shop. By comparison, the atmosphere in here seems as delicate as one of the ancient East Asian porcelains on display. Hold your breath and get an eyeful of furniture, 18th-century Japanese woodblock prints, and a world-class collection of Chinese and Japanese textiles. There are also scrolls, screens, engravings, and lacquers.

✪ **A Gallery for Fine Photography.** 322 Royal St. ☎ **504/568-1313.** Mon–Sat 10am–6pm, Sun 11am–6pm.

It would be a mistake to skip this incredibly well-stocked photography gallery. It really is like a museum of photography, with just about every period and style represented, and frequent shows of contemporary artists. The gallery emphasizes New Orleans and Southern history and contemporary culture (you can buy Ernest Belloq's legendary Storyville photos) as well as black culture and music. There is something in just about every price range, as well as a terrific collection of photography books.

Hanson Gallery. 229 Royal St. ☎ **504/524-8211.** Mon–Sat 10am–6pm, Sun 11am–5pm.

Hanson Gallery shows paintings, sculpture, and limited-edition prints by contemporary artists such as Peter Max, Frederick Hart, Pradzynski, Anoro, Thysell, Deckbar, Zjawinska, Erickson, LeRoy Neiman, Richard MacDonald, and Behrens.

Kurt E. Schon, Ltd. 510 St. Louis St. and 523 Royal St. ☎ **504/524-5462.** Mon–Sat 9am–5pm.

Here you'll find the country's largest inventory of 19th-century European paintings. Works include French and British Impressionist and post-Impressionist paintings as well as art from the Royal Academy and the French Salon.

LeMieux Galleries. 332 Julia St. ☎ **504/522-5988.** Mon–Sat 10am–5:30pm.

LeMieux represents contemporary artists and fine craftspeople from Louisiana and the Gulf Coast.

Mario Villa. 3908 Magazine St. ☎ **504/895-8731.** Mon 11–5pm, Tues–Sat 10am–5pm.

Mario Villa is New Orleans' undisputed king of design, or at least the city's most ubiquitous designer. There are canvas rugs; plush sofas; wrought-iron chairs, lamps, and tables with organic twists and turns; and a liberal spray of photographs and paintings.

New Orleans School of Glassworks and Printmaking Studio. 727 Magazine St. ☎ **504/529-7277.** Mon–Sat 11am–5pm. Closed Sat July–Aug.

Established glasswork artists and master printmakers display their work in the on-site gallery and teach classes in glassblowing, kiln-fired glass, hand-engraved printmaking, papermaking, and book-binding. Absolutely unique to the area, the place is worth a visit during gallery hours. Daily glassblowing, fusing, and slumping demonstrations are open for viewing.

✪ **Peligro.** 305 Decatur St. ☎ **504/581-1706.** Mon–Thurs 10am–6pm, Fri–Sat 10am–10pm, Sun noon–6pm.

A bit out of the way but worth checking out, Peligro is one of the best folk art galleries in the city, with an emphasis on primitive and outsider art (but also work from Latin American countries).

The Rodrigue Gallery of New Orleans. 721 Royal St. ☎ **504/581-4244.** Daily 10am–6pm.

Blue Dog is the Freddie Krueger of New Orleans; once you've seen Cajun artist George Rodrique's creation, it invades your consciousness and torments your life. Oh, the staring, otherwordly, bordering-on-kitsch canine has its fans, but it scares us. This gallery is the source for all your Blue Dog needs.

Still–Zinsel Contemporary Fine Art. 328 Julia St. ☎ **504/588-9999.** Mon–Sat 10am–5pm.

This fine art gallery shows paintings, sculpture, photography, and works on paper by contemporary local, national, and international artists. If you're hopping along gallery row on Julia Street, be sure to hop in here; it regularly shows some of the best work on the strip.

BOOKS

Literary enthusiasts will find many destinations in New Orleans. **Maple Street Book Shop,** 7523 Maple St. (☎ **504/866-4916**), is an uptown mecca for bookworms; the **Maple Street Children's Book Shop** is next door at 7529 Maple St. (☎ **504/861-2105**), and **Beaucoup Books** is at 5414 Magazine St. (☎ **504/895-2663**). **Little Professor Book Center of New Orleans,** 1000 S. Carrollton Ave. (☎ **504/866-7646**), stocks one of the best general selections.

Beckham's Bookshop. 228 Decatur St. ☎ **504/522-9875.** Daily 10am–6pm.

Beckham's has two entire floors of old editions, rare secondhand books, and thousands of classical LPs that will tie up your whole afternoon or morning if you don't tear yourself away. The owners also operate **Librairie Bookshop,** 823 Chartres St. (☎ **504/525-4837**), which has a sizable collection of secondhand books.

Faubourg Marigny Bookstore. 600 Frenchmen St. ☎ **504/943-9875.** Mon–Fri 10am–8pm, Sat–Sun 10am–6pm.

This well-stocked gay and lesbian bookstore also carries some local titles and holds regular readings and signings.

✪ **Faulkner House Books.** 624 Pirates Alley. ☎ **504/524-2940.** Daily 10am–6pm.

This shop is on a lot of walking tours of the French Quarter, because it's where Nobel Prize–winner William Faulkner lived while he was writing his early works *Mosquitoes* and *Soldiers' Pay.* Inside is possibly the best selection per square foot of any bookstore in the whole world, with every bit of shelf space occupied by a book that's both highly collectible and of literary value. The shop holds a large collection of Faulkner first editions and rare and first-edition classics by many other authors, and has a particularly comprehensive collection of New Orleans–related work.

✪ **Garden District Book Shop.** 2727 Prytania St. (in the Rink). ☎ **504/ 895-2266.** Mon–Sat 10am–6pm, Sun 11am–4pm.

The two best bookstores in town dealing in new books are Faulkner's, downtown, and this uptown favorite. Owner Britton Trice has stocked his medium-sized shop with just about every regional book you can think of. This is also the place where Anne Rice does book signings whenever she has a new release.

George Herget Books. 3109 Magazine St. ☎ **504/891-5595.** Mon–Sat 10am–5:30pm, Sun 11am–5pm.

George Herget Books is another of New Orleans' great bookstores. More than 20,000 rare and used books covering absolutely every subject imaginable await browsers and collectors.

CANDIES & PRALINES

✪ **Laura's Candies.** 600 Conti St. ☎ **800/992-9699** or 504/525-3880. Daily 10am–7pm.

Laura's is said to be New Orleans' oldest candy store, established in 1913. It has fabulous pralines, but it also has rich, delectable golf-ball-sized truffles—our personal favorite indulgence.

✪ **Leah's Candy Kitchen.** 714 St. Louis St. ☎ **504/523-5662.** Mon–Sat 10am–10pm, Sun 10am–6pm.

After you've tried all of New Orleans' Creole candy shops, you might very well come to the conclusion that Leah's tops the list. Everything here, from the candy fillings to the chocolate-covered pecan brittle, is made from scratch by second- and third-generation members of Leah Johnson's praline-cookin' family.

COSTUMES & MASKS

Costumery is big business in New Orleans, and not just in the days before Lent. A number of shops in the city specialize in props for Mardi Gras, Halloween, and other occasions. In New Orleans, you never know when you're going to want or need a costume.

✪ **Little Shop of Fantasy.** 523 Dumaine St. ☎ **504/529-4243.** Mon–Tues and Thurs–Sat 10am–6pm, Sun 1–6pm.

In the Little Shop of Fantasy, owners Mike Stark, Laura and Anne Guccione, and Jill Kellys sell the work of a number of local artists and more than 20 mask makers. Mike creates the feathered masks, Jill does the velvet hats and costumes, and Laura and Anne produce homemade toiletries.

Mardi Gras Center. 831 Chartres St. ☎ **504/524-4384.** Mon–Sat 10am–5pm, Sun 10am–3pm.

Mardi Gras Center carries sizes 2 to 50 and has a wide selection of new, ready-made costumes as well as used outfits. It also carries accessories, such as beads, doubloons, wigs, masks, hats, makeup, jewelry, and Mardi Gras decorations. Mardi Gras Center is also a good place to stop for Halloween supplies.

Uptown Costume & Dance Company. 5533 Magazine St. ☎ **504/895-7969.** Tues–Sat 10am–6pm.

The walls of this small store are covered with spooky monster masks, goofy arrow-through-the-head-type tricks, hats, wigs, makeup, and all other manner of playfulness. At Mardi Gras, though, things really get cooking. The shop designs party uniforms for a number of Mardi Gras krewe members.

FASHION

The Grace Note. 900 Royal St. ☎ **504/522-1513.** Mon–Sat 10am–6pm, Sun 11am–5pm.

Primarily a clothing store, Grace Note also features some gifts. It's a bit pricey, but the clothes are stunning. The designers here work with vintage and new materials, and what they come up with is usually lush, memorable, and very touchable.

Jazz Rags. 1215 Decatur St. ☎ **504/523-2942.** Thurs–Mon noon–6pm.

Stuffed full of stylish, upscale, but reasonably priced, men's and women's vintage clothes. You can find locals combing the racks here for Mardi Gras and Halloween costumes.

Jim Smiley Fine Vintage Clothing. 2001 Magazine St. ☎ **504/528-9449.** Daily 11am–5pm.

Jim Smiley has attracted national media recognition as one of the best shops in the world. It features exceptional men's and women's attire, accessories, linens, and textiles from the 19th and 20th centuries.

Trashy Diva. 829 Chartres St. ☎ **504/581-4555.** Mon–Sat noon–6pm, Sun 1–6pm.

Despite the name, there is nothing trashy about the vintage clothes found here. They are absolute treasures, not the usual hit-and-miss bulk found at other vintage shops, unique and in terrific shape, dating from the turn of the century to the 1960s. The drawback is that you will pay through the nose for them.

FOOD & DRINK

Café du Monde Coffee Shop. 800 Decatur St. ☎ **504/581-2914.** Daily 24 hours.

If you want to try your hand at making those scrumptious New Orleans beignets, you can buy the mix at the Café du Monde, in the French Market. To make it complete, pick up a can of the cafe's famous coffee, a special blend of coffee and chicory. The shop also has a very good mail-order service (☎ 800/772-2927; fax 504/587-0847).

Creole Delicacies Gourmet Shop. Riverwalk Marketplace. ☎ **504/523-6425.** www.cookingcajun.com. Mon–Sat 10am–9pm, Sun 10am–7pm.

You'll find Cajun and Creole packaged foods and mixes here. Fill your shopping basket with everything from jambalaya and gumbo mix to rémoulade and hot sauces. There's another branch of Creole Delicacies at 533 St. Ann St. (☎ 504/525-9508).

Martin Wine Cellar. 3827 Baronne St. ☎ **504/899-7411.** Mon–Sat 10am–7pm, Sun 10am–2pm.

If you're a wine lover or connoisseur—or if you want to become one—Martin Wine Cellar may be your most significant find in New Orleans.

Orleans Coffee Exchange. 712 Orleans Ave. ☎ **504/522-5710.** www.orleanscoffee.com. Mon–Fri 8am–6pm, Sat–Sun 9am–6pm.

Java junkies should know about the Orleans Coffee Exchange. The 500 varieties of coffee beans here come from all over the world. There are also more than 350 flavored coffees, as well as scores of exotic teas.

GIFTS

Accent Annex Mardi Gras Headquarters. 633 Toulose. ☎ **504/592-9886.** 10am–6pm daily.

Need some Mardi Gras beads, masks, and other accoutrements? This is one of the biggest suppliers of such things, and has just about everything you need to properly celebrate Mardi Gras in New Orleans, or to stock up for that party you want to throw back home.

Artifacts. 5515 Magazine St. ☎ **504/899-5505.** Mon–Sat 11am–5pm.

This gallery and shop is an eye feast, featuring finely crafted one-of-a-kind furniture, lamps, mirrors, and jewelry by local and national artists. There is also a nice selection of decorative hardware.

Casa del Corazon. 901 Chartres St. ☎ **504/569-9555.** Daily 10am–5pm

Gifts, sundries, and folk arts "from the warm latitudes" with an emphasis on Latin America are here, with some Spanish, Italian, and African items.

Living Room. 927 Royal St. ☎ **504/595-8860.** Mon–Sat 10am–6pm, Sun noon–6pm.

The fine job the friendly owner has done here with her original folk craft store almost makes up for the loss of the site's former occupant, the beloved Olive Book Store. Living Room holds an eclectic assortment of old and new furnishings, knickknacks (think frames made of wood from old plantations, old spoons, and other recycled materials), fine art, and antiques.

Orient Expressed Imports. 3906 Magazine St. ☎ **504/899-3060.** www.orientexpressed.com Mon–Sat 10am–5pm.

This shop features a fascinating collection of antiques, santos, and objets d'art from around the world. The shop also offers its own line of hand-smocked children's clothing, plus toys and gifts.

Scriptura. 5423 Magazine St. ☎ **888/263-9699** or 504/897-1555. Mon–Sat 10am–6pm.

This store has everything related to the elegant art of scribbling—it's been said that the owners here love paper more than life itself. You can get designer stationery, glass fountain pens, sealing wax and wax presses, and all types of generic or specific (travel, cigar, wine, restaurant) journals.

Thomas Mann Gallery. 1804 Magazine St. ☎ **504/581-2113.** Mon–Sat 11am–6pm.

This is a design store conceived by "techno-romantic" jewelry designer Thomas Mann. It aims at "redefining contemporary living" with its eclectic collection of jewelry, lighting, and home furnishings. They also have another location at 829 Royal St. in the French Quarter.

HATS

Meyer the Hatter. 120 St. Charles Ave. ☎ **800/882-4287** or 504/525-1048. www.neworleans.com/meyer. Mon–Sat 10am–5:45pm.

Meyer's opened more than 100 years ago and has been in the same family since. Today, the haberdashery has one of the largest selections of fine hats and caps in the South. Men will find distinguished international labels like Stetson, Kangol, Akubra, Dobbs, and Borsalino (and there are some hats for women as well). The store is 1 block off Canal Street.

MUSIC

In addition to the giant **Tower Records** at 408 N. Peters St. (☎ 504/529-4411), there are a few other places you should check out for music, especially if you still have a turntable.

✪ **Louisiana Music Factory.** 210 Decatur St. ☎ **504/586-1094.** Daily 10am–10pm.

This popular store carries a large selection of regional music—including Cajun, zydeco, R&B, jazz, blues, and gospel—plus books, posters, and T-shirts. It also has frequent live music and beer bashes—shop while you bop!

Record Ron's. 239 Chartres St. ☎ **800/234-6889** or 504/522-2239. Daily 11am–7pm.

At Record Ron's you'll find thousands of 45s, CDs, and cassettes, plus a good selection of LPs covering classic rock, jazz, Cajun, zydeco, R&B, and blues. T-shirts, posters, sheet music, rubber stamps, music memorabilia, and jewelry are also available.

Rock & Roll Records & Collectibles. 1214 Decatur St. ☎ **504/561-5683.**
www.neworleans.com/rock-n-roll. Daily 10am–10pm.

> The name says it all—kind of. This is record nerd heaven. The walls
> are lined with classics, and floor space is at a minimum thanks to
> boxes and crates full of records. Prices are negotiable.

THE OCCULT

The Bottom of the Cup Tearoom. 732 Royal St. ☎ **504/523-1204.** Mon–
Fri 10am–6pm, Sat–Sun 11am–7pm.

> At the Bottom of the Cup Tearoom, psychics and clairvoyants spe-
> cialize in palm reading, crystal gazing, tea-leaf reading, and tarot.
> You can also get your astrological chart done. It's been open since
> 1929 and bills itself as the "oldest tearoom in the United States."

Marie Laveau's House of Voodoo. 739 Bourbon St. ☎ **888/4-VOODOO**
or 504/581-3751. Sun–Thurs 10am–11:30pm, Fri–Sat 10am–12:30 or 1:30am.

> The place for all your voodoo doll and gris-gris bag needs. Tourist
> voodoo, to be sure, but such items make great souvenirs for the right
> friends, and it's a fun store to poke around in.

Westgate—The Original Necrotorium. 5219 Magazine St. ☎ **504/
899-3077.** Tues–Sat noon–5pm.

> Painted a hard-to-miss purple and black, this is the ultimate store
> for the right-minded visitor, and a complete nightmare (deliberately)
> for others. Even if you aren't a death-o-phile, it's interesting to
> browse through, but it might give some the creeps.

UMBRELLAS

The Umbrella Lady. 1107 Decatur St. ☎ **504/523-7791.** Daily 10am–8pm.

She's called "The Umbrella Lady," but her real name is Anne B.
Lane. You'll find her in her upstairs studio, above Molly's at the
Market bar. A Quarter fixture, she's the creator of wonderful
Secondline umbrellas as well as fanciful "Southern belle" parasols.
Look for the umbrellas displayed on her balcony.

8

New Orleans After Dark

*N*ew Orleans is one of the most beautiful cities in the United States, possibly the world, but we won't mind if you never see a bit of it—provided, however, that the omission is because you are spending the daylight sightseeing hours recovering from the equally extraordinary nightlife.

This is a city of music and rhythm. It is impossible to imagine New Orleans without a soundtrack of jazz, Cajun, and zydeco. Music pours out of every doorway, and sometimes it seems people are dancing down the street. Sometimes they are. (After all, this is the town that sends you to your grave with music and then dances back from the cemetery.) You walk along Bourbon Street, for example, and with every step, you hear music of all varieties. Maybe none of it is world class, but that doesn't seem to matter too much. It's just that it's there at all, and in such variety. Plus, it's darn infectious.

Virtually every night, dozens of clubs all over town offer music that can range from average to extraordinary, but is never less than danceable. In most places, cover prices vary from night to night and performer to performer, but rarely will you have to pay more than $10, and then only for more high-falutin' places like the House of Blues. When the clubs get too full, no matter; the crowd spills into the street, talking, drinking, and still dancing right there on the sidewalk (the music is often plenty audible out there). Sometimes the action outside is even more fun than inside, not to mention less hot and sweaty. Club hopping is easy, though with some exceptions some of the better choices will require leaving the Quarter. Don't worry—most are a cheap cab ride away, and many are within an additional, even cheaper cab ride, if not walking distance, of each other. We strongly urge you to leave the Quarter at night to visit some of the town's better joints. However, if you aren't up to that, don't fret. Several of the best jazz and brass band clubs are right in the Quarter. And only steps away is the scene in the Frenchmen section of the Faubourg Marigny, where at least five clubs are going at once, within 3 blocks of each other. People wander from one to the other, sometimes never bothering to actually pay the cover price and go inside. If you do your evening right, those calories you consumed all day long will be gone by morning.

Or, yes, you could spend your night running from bar to bar. There is no lack. With such great music available, that seems a waste of time; if all you wanted to do was drink, you could have stayed home and enjoyed yourself just as much. Still, it is New Orleans, and some of these places are as convivial and atmospheric as you will ever find; ducking into a few isn't a bad idea at all. And of course, everything only gets livelier and wilder as the evening goes on.

And speaking of which, don't be fooled by the times given in local listings for band performances. If it says "10pm," the band will probably go on closer to midnight and keep playing until late. Really late. Chances are good that if you come late, even really late, you will still catch quite a bit of the act you came to see.

For up-to-date information on what's happening around town, look for current editions of *Gambit, Offbeat,* and *Where,* all distributed free in most hotels and all record stores. You can also check out *Offbeat* on the Internet (www.nola.com; once you get to the Nola home page, go to the music and entertainment section). Other sources include the *Times-Picayune's* daily entertainment calendar and Friday's "Lagniappe" section of the newspaper. Additionally, **WWOZ** (90.7 FM) broadcasts the local music schedule several times throughout the day. If you miss the broadcasts, call ☎ **504/840-4040,** WWOZ's "Tower Records Second Line," for the same information.

1 Jazz & Blues Clubs

This being New Orleans, jazz and blues are everywhere—though not all of it is worth hearing. Not that any of it is bad, per se. It's just that there is world-class stuff out there competing with tourist traps for your ears, so don't just settle for the first sight (or sound) of brass instruments.

THE FRENCH QUARTER & THE FAUBOURG MARIGNY

✪ **Donna's.** 800 N. Rampart St. ☎ **504/596-6914.** Cover varies according to performer.

A corner bar at the edge of the Quarter, Donna's has become one of the top spots for the revival of the brass band experience and for a variety of jazz and blues traditions. As with most real New Orleans hangouts, atmosphere is minimal, but spirits (liquid and otherwise) are high. The cover charge for performances is usually no more than the cost of a good mixed drink. Well worth a stop on an evening of club hopping.

Dragon's Den. 435 Esplanade Ave. (above Siam Café). ☎ **504/949-1750.** Cover $4–$10.

Imagine a hippie-cum-opium den turned performance space and you'll have an idea of the Dragon's Den. Before show time, it's a pillows-on-the-floor, nouvelle Asian restaurant. After the lights go down, however, the place transforms into one of the funkiest jazz venues in the city.

Fritzel's European Jazz Pub. 733 Bourbon St. ☎ **504/561-0432.** No cover; 1-drink minimum per set.

You might walk right past this small establishment, but that would be a big mistake, because this 1831 building brings some of the city's best musicians to play on its tiny stage. In addition to the regular weekend program of late-night jazz (Friday and Saturday from 10:30pm, Sunday from 10pm), there are frequent jam sessions in the wee hours during the week, when performers end their stints elsewhere and gather to play "Musicians' Music."

Funky Butt. 714 N. Rampart St. ☎ **504/558-0872.** Cover varies.

Fret not—this is not a strip bar. Downstairs is a typical funky bar; upstairs is a slightly more pleasing and mature performance space than that at other clubs in town. It's leaning toward, if not totally achieving, smoky jazz nightclub ambience. Bookings emphasize jazz but can also include anything from the Wild Magnolias (the most famous of the Mardi Gras Indians) to an amazing Billie Holiday tribute band to the New Orleans Klezmer All Stars. *Note:* Although the club itself is safe, the neighborhood around it isn't. Take a cab (yes, it seems silly, but even from Bourbon Street).

Funky Pirate. 727 Bourbon St. ☎ **504/523-1960.** 1-drink minimum.

Decorated to resemble a pirates' den, the Funky Pirate lives up to its name. The place seems to be perpetually full of loud beer-drinkers, and at night it can get jam-packed. "Big" Al Carson and the Blues Masters hold court here, playing live blues.

John Wehner's Famous Door. 339 Bourbon St. ☎ **504/522-7626.** 1-drink minimum per set. Occasional cover.

Open since 1934, the Famous Door is the oldest music club on Bourbon Street. At night, the John Wehner's Dream Band offers a tourist-crowd pleasing selection of Motown, funk and swing.

French Quarter Nightlife

Esplanade Ave.
Barracks St.
Gov. Nicholls St.
Ursulines St.
St. Philip St.
Dumaine St.
Madison St.
St. Ann St.
Orleans St.
St. Peter St.
Toulouse St.
Wilk Row
St. Louis St.
Conti St.
Bienville St.
Exchange Alley

N. Rampart St.
Burgundy St.
Dauphine St.
Bourbon St.
Royal St.
Chartres St.
Decatur St.
N. Peters St.
Clinton St.
N. Peter's St.

Louis Armstrong Park
Jackson Square
Moonwalk
Mississippi River
Woldenberg Park
French Market Pl.

Apple Barrel **7**
Beque's at the Royal Sonesta **32**
Bombay Club **51**
Bourbon Pub—Parade Disco **18**
Café Brasil **8**
Café Lafitte in Exile **16**
Carousel Bar & Lounge **36**
Checkpoint Charlie's **6**
Chris Owens Club **29**
Crescent City Brewhouse **27**
Donna's **2**
Dragon's Den **6**
Dream Palace **8**
Feelings **9**
Fritzel's European Jazz Pub **20**
Funky Butt **3**
Funky Pirate **21**
Golden Lantern **10**
Good Friends Bar & Queens Head Pub **19**
Hard Rock Cafe **40**
House of Blues **37**
Jimmy Buffet's Margaritaville Cafe & Storyville Tavern **14**

John Wehner's Famous Door **35**
Kerry Irish Pub **39**
Lafitte's Blacksmith Shop **15**
LeRoundup **30**
Levon Helm's Classic American Cafe **38**
Maison Bourbon **22**
Napolean House Bar & Cafe **28**
O'Flaherty's Irish Channel Pub **27**
Oz **17**
Palm Court Jazz Café **13**
Pat O'Brien's **24**
Planet Hollywood **26**
Preservation Hall **23**
R Bar and Royal Street Inn **5**
Rawhide **4**
Rick's Cabaret **34**
Rubyfruit Jungle **11**
Shim-Sham Club **25**
Snug Harbor **12**
Storyville **33**
Tipitina's French Quarter **41**
Wolfendale's **1**

NA-0073

Maison Bourbon. 641 Bourbon St. ☎ **504/522-8818.** 1-drink minimum.

Despite its location, Maison Bourbon is not a tourist trap. The music is very authentic, and often superb, jazz. From about midafternoon until the wee hours, Dixieland and traditional jazz hold forth, often at loud and lively volume.

Palm Court Jazz Café. 1204 Decatur St. ☎ **504/525-0200.** Cover $5 per person at tables; no cover at bar.

This is one of the most stylish jazz haunts in the Quarter. It's an elegant setting in which to catch top-notch jazz groups Wednesday through Sunday. The music varies nightly, but is generally traditional or classic jazz.

Praline Connection Gospel & Blues Hall. 907 S. Peters St. ☎ **504/523-3973** for reservations and information.

The 9,000-square-foot Praline Connection Gospel & Blues Hall is a soul-food restaurant serving live music with dinner on Thursday, Friday, and Saturday nights. Sunday brings a great gospel buffet brunch. Reservations are strongly recommended.

✪ **Preservation Hall.** 726 St. Peter St. ☎ **504/522-2841,** or 504/523-8939 after 8pm. Cover $4.

This is an essential spot for anyone coming to New Orleans. It doesn't get any more authentic than this. With no seats, terrible sight lines, and constant crowds, you won't be able to see much, but you won't care, because you will be having too much fun and a cheerfully sweaty time. Even if you don't consider yourself interested in jazz, there is a seriously good time to be had here. Patrons start lining up at 6:15—the doors open at 8pm, so the trick to avoid the line is to get there either just as the doors open, or later in the evening.

✪ **Snug Harbor.** 626 Frenchmen St. ☎ **504/949-0696.** www.snugjazz.com. Cover $8–$20, depending on performer.

If your idea of jazz extends beyond Dixieland, and if you prefer a concert-type setting over a messy nightclub, get your hands on Snug Harbor's monthly schedule. On the fringes of the French Quarter (1 block beyond Esplanade Avenue), Snug Harbor is the city's premier showcase for contemporary jazz, with a few blues and R&B combos thrown in for good measure. You should buy tickets in advance.

Storyville District. 125 Bourbon St. ☎ **504/410-1000.** Daily 11:30am–2am. Music noon–3pm and 5pm–2am. No cover.

This is the brand-new brainchild of (in part) Quint Davis, the man who helps brings us Jazz Fest every year. The idea is to bring high-quality jazz back to Bourbon Street, in a nonfrat party atmosphere. Music plays much of the day, starting in the red-walled parlor room in the afternoon, with bigger bands playing in a larger, more clublike space at night.

OUTSIDE THE FRENCH QUARTER

The New Showcase Lounge. 1915 N. Broad St. ☎ **504/945-5612.** Cover varies.

Even though it has the patina of an age-old joint, this is one of the newest clubs in town, and the music it showcases is modern jazz with an occasional blues singer. It's in the same family of clubs with Snug Harbor, only a little looser, and it is another place to look for members of the Marsalis clan.

Pete Fountain's. In the New Orleans Hilton, 2 Poydras St. ☎ **504/523-4374** or 504/561-0500. Cover $19 (includes 1 drink).

Pete Fountain has managed to make his name synonymous with New Orleans music. He grew up playing around town, moved to Chicago with the Dukes of Dixieland, joined Lawrence Welk's orchestra, and then, for more than 20 years, held forth in his own Bourbon Street club. These days you'll find him here. Pete is featured in one show a night, Tuesday to Saturday at 10pm. You'll need reservations.

✪ **The Red Room.** 2040 St. Charles Ave. ☎ **504/528-9759.** Jacket and tie recommended for men. No cover.

Swing has finally caught on in New Orleans, with a vengeance, helped no doubt in part by this hot, fairly new, '40s-style jazz and supper club. Live music happens every night, with jazz and swing performed by both established names and talented up and comers. It's a lively place, perfect for dancing and romancing.

Vaughn's Lounge. 800 Lesseps St. ☎ **504/947-5562.** Cover varies.

Tucked deep in the Bywater section of New Orleans, Vaughn's Lounge feels almost as though you're in someone's house. Thursday—Kermit Ruffin's night—is the night to go to Vaughn's. Be sure to take a taxi.

2 Cajun & Zydeco Joints

Most of the so-called Cajun joints in New Orleans are really Cajun for tourists, in both sound and setting. If you want the real thing,

New Orleans Nightlife

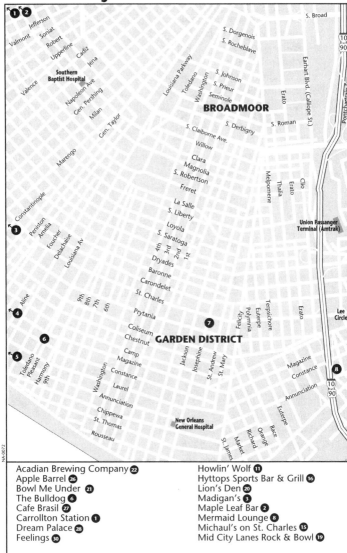

Acadian Brewing Company ㉒
Apple Barrel ㉖
Bowl Me Under ㉑
The Bulldog ⑥
Cafe Brasil ㉗
Carrollton Station ①
Dream Palace ㉘
Feelings ㉚

Howlin' Wolf ⑪
Hyttops Sports Bar & Grill ⑯
Lion's Den ⑳
Madigan's ③
Maple Leaf Bar ②
Mermaid Lounge ⑧
Michaul's on St. Charles ⑮
Mid City Lanes Rock & Bowl ⑲

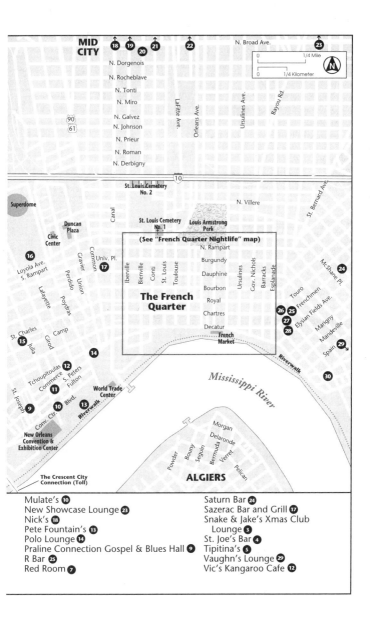

MID CITY

N. Broad Ave.

N. Dorgenois
N. Rocheblave
N. Tonti
N. Miro
N. Galvez
N. Johnson
N. Prieur
N. Roman
N. Derbigny

LaFitte Ave.
Orleans Ave.
Ursulines Ave.
Bayou Rd.

0   1/4 Mile
0   1/4 Kilometer

Superdome

St. Louis Cemetery No. 2

St. Louis Cemetery No. 1

Louis Armstrong Park

N. Villere

St. Bernard Ave.

Duncan Plaza

Civic Center

Loyola Ave.
S. Rampart
Gravier
Common
Univ. Pl.

(See "French Quarter Nightlife" map)

N. Rampart
Burgundy
Dauphine
Bourbon
Royal
Chartres
Decatur

Iberville
Bienville
Conti
St. Louis
Toulouse

Ursulines
Gov. Nichols
Barracks
Esplanade

The French Quarter

Touro
Frenchmen
Elysian Fields Ave.
Mangny
Mandeville
Spain

McShane Pl.

Lafayette
Perdido
Poydras
Union
Girod
Camp
Julia

St. Charles

Tchoupitoulas
Commerce
S. Peters
Fulton

St. Joseph
Conv. Ctr. Blvd.
Riverwalk

World Trade Center

French Market

Mississippi River

Riverwalk

New Orleans Convention & Exhibition Center

The Crescent City Connection (Toll)

Morgan
Delaronde
Bermuda
Verret
Pelican
Powder
Bounty
Seguin

ALGIERS

Mulate's 🔟
New Showcase Lounge ㉓
Nick's 🔞
Pete Fountain's ⓭
Polo Lounge ⓮
Praline Connection Gospel & Blues Hall ⑨
Red Room ⑦

Saturn Bar ㉔
Sazerac Bar and Grill ⓱
Snake & Jake's Xmas Club Lounge ③
St. Joe's Bar ④
Tipitina's ⑤
Vaughn's Lounge ㉙
Vic's Kangaroo Cafe ⓬

141

you are better off going out to bayou country. Which is not to say some of the finest Cajun bands don't play in New Orleans—it's just that you are likely to find, say, the world-renowned Beausoleil at the Maple Leaf or the Grammy-nominated Hackberry Ramblers at the Mermaid Lounge, neither of which is a Cajun club. What these spots do offer is a place to learn to Cajun dance, which is a skill that comes in handy in New Orleans.

Michaul's on St. Charles. 840 St. Charles Ave. ☎ **504/522-5517.** No cover.

Michaul's attempts to re-create the Cajun dance hall experience, and for a prefab kind of place, it does it well enough. Come for the free dance lessons.

✪ **Mid City Lanes Rock & Bowl.** 4133 S. Carrollton Ave. ☎ **504/482-3133.** www.cajunmarket.com/rock_n_bowl.html. Bowling: daytime and Sun–Thurs evening $8 per hour; Fri–Sat evening $10 per hour. Show admission $5–$7.

Everything we just said about tourist traps and nonauthentic experiences does not apply here. It does not get any more authentic than a club set in the middle of a bowling alley, which is itself set in the middle of a strip mall. It's the best place for zydeco, particularly on the nights devoted to Zydeco Wars, when the audience votes on whether, say, Boozoo Chavis or Beau Jacque is the King of Zydeco.

Mulate's. 201 Julia St. (at Convention Center Blvd.). ☎ **504/522-1492.** No cover.

A branch of the original out in Cajun country and a not-unlikely place to find authentic, and decent, Cajun bands. The stage and dance area are relatively spacious, and the food isn't bad.

3 Rhythm, Rock & the Rest of the Music Scene

Most clubs in New Orleans feature an eclectic lineup that reflects the town's music scene; even the local papers refer to club lineups as "mixed bags." If you want a specific sound, you have to look at listings (in *Offbeat* and *Gambit* magazines, for example) night by night. Some places are generally good fun on their own, regardless of who is playing; any night at the **Maple Leaf** is going to be a good one, while wandering from spot to spot in the Frenchmen section is a well-spent evening.

THE FRENCH QUARTER & THE FAUBOURG MARIGNY

Cafe Brasil. 2100 Chartres St. ☎ **504/949-0851.** Cover varies according to performer.

Day (when it is a great place to get a cup of coffee and hear gossip) or night (when it delivers danceable music), Cafe Brasil is the center of the increasingly lively and popular Frenchmen section of the Faubourg Marigny. It features Latin or Caribbean music, R&B, or jazz almost every night, and chances are whatever is playing will be infectious.

Checkpoint Charlie's. 501 Esplanade Ave. ☎ **504/949-7012.** No cover.

Somewhere between a biker bar and a college hangout, the dark Checkpoint Charlie's only seems intimidating—though the hard rock sounds usually blaring from the stage help. R&B and blues sneak into the mix, as well as the occasional acoustic open-mike night.

Dream Palace. 534 Frenchmen St. ☎ **504/945-2040.** Cover varies; usually $4.

Dream Palace's decor is nothing special, but its varied schedule of Latin music, rock, R&B, and blues makes it a worthwhile stop on the Frenchmen tour. Crowds tend to be young, but well beyond college age.

✪ **House of Blues.** 225 Decatur St. ☎ **504/529-2583.** Cover $5–$25.

New Orleans was a natural place for this franchise to set up shop, but its presence in the French Quarter seems rather unnatural. That isn't to say the Disney-like facility is without its qualities. The music room has adequate sight lines and good sound, and the chain's financial muscle assures first-rate bookings, from local legends like the Neville Brothers to such ace out-of-towners as Los Lobos and Nanci Griffith.

Levon Helm's Classic American Cafe. 300 Dectaur. ☎ **504/522-5907.** Cover $5–$20 (though if you arrive before 8pm, it's free).

Don't let the clunky name, which puts one in mind of the dreaded "theme" restaurants, fool you. It is clear they are genuinely passionate about music, particularly New Orleans rock and R&B. The legendary Irma Thomas has made the cafe her French Quarter home, and oh, yes, The Band plays, too.

Shim-Sham Club. 615 Toulouse St. ☎ **504/565-5400.** Cover varies.

Taking over a longtime jazz club space, the new Shim-Sham only does about eight shows a month (at this writing), and its bar setting (definitely not a dive) has a good vibe. Booking is somewhat of a mixed bag, but tends toward roots, rockabilly, and swing.

Tipitina's French Quarter. 233 N. Peters St. ☎ **504/891-8477.** www.
tipitinas.com. Cover varies.

By gosh, they pretty much took the original Tip's, shrunk it down
and stuck it in the French Quarter. Good for them. Unlike other
(admittedly) tourist-geared spots, this has some ring of authenticity
and so it is a most welcome addition to the Quarter. Great shows
are frequent, and regular features include Sunday BBQ and swing
sessions with Kermit Ruffins, and Friday and Saturday Happy Hour
(5 to 8pm) with New Orleans piano great Eddie Bo.

Tipitina's Ruins. 1101 Convention Center Blvd. ☎ **504/895-8477.** Cover
varies.

Taking the place of the late and not lamented Tip's Big Room, this
is another attempt (only just opened at press time) by the venerable
club to run a big space for semi-occasional large concerts (the Neville
Brothers, Isaac Hayes, the Funky Meters).

OUTSIDE THE FRENCH QUARTER

Throughout this book, we keep nagging you to be sure to leave the
Quarter. At no time is this as important as at night. There are so
many terrific clubs elsewhere. They aren't hard to find—any cab
driver knows where they are. And not only do they feature some of
the best music in town (if not, on some nights, in the country), but
they aren't designed as tourist destinations, so your experience will
be that much more enjoyable.

Bowl Me Under. 4133 S. Carrollton Ave. ☎ **504/482-3133.**

Located right under the Mid City Lanes—hence the name—this is
a huge room that helps take care of the constant overflow from upstairs. Bowl Me Under offers essentially the same acts as Mid City,
though perhaps not as much zydeco. On some nights, the clubs split
the bill—pay one price, see two bands, one upstairs and one downstairs—sometimes leading to strange, or not so, combinations of acts.

Carrollton Station. 8140 Willow St. ☎ **504/865-9190.** Cover $3–$10.

Way uptown in the Riverbend area, Carrollton Station is a gourmet
beer house that schedules local and touring blues, classic New Orleans, and R&B musicians (plus some singer-songwriter types)
Wednesday through Sunday, generally beginning at 10pm. (The bar
opens at 3pm.)

✪ **Howlin' Wolf.** 828 S. Peters St. ☎ **504/523-2551.** Cover none–$15.

This is arguably the premier club in town in the quality and fame
of its bookings, thanks to a remodeling job that increased capacity

nearly fourfold—and made it a competitor with the former House of Blues powerhouse. Howlin' Wolf draws some top touring rock acts, though it is not at all limited to rock—El Vez, the Mexican Elvis, is as likely to play as a country band or the latest in indie and alternative.

Lion's Den. 2655 Gravier St. ☎ **504/821-3745.** Cover varies.

A true neighborhood dive, but well worth stopping by should Miss Irma Thomas be in residence. She usually is, and sometimes, if you're lucky, she's even cooking up some red beans and rice. Thomas has only one hit to her credit ("Wish Somebody Would Care"), but she's still a great, sassy live R&B and soul act with a devoted following.

✪ **Maple Leaf Bar.** 8316 Oak St. ☎ **504/866-9359.** Cover $3–$10, depending on day of week and performer.

This is what a New Orleans club is all about. It's medium-sized, but feels smaller when a crowd is packed in. More often than not, the crowd spills onto the sidewalk and into the street to dance and drink. If Beausoleil or the ReBirth Brass Band is playing, do not miss it; go and dance till you drop.

Mermaid Lounge. 1102 Constance St. ☎ **504/524-4747.** Cover none–$10.

Although it's very hard, it's worth the effort. An eclectic booking policy means everything from the Hackberry Ramblers (the Grammy-nominated Cajun band that has been playing together for nearly 70 years!) to hard-core grunge—and yet, the blue-haired pierced kids still come to dance to the Cajun bands in the tiny, cramped, dark, L-shaped space. One of the coolest vibes in town.

Tipitina's. 501 Napoleon Ave. ☎ **504/895-8477,** or 504/897-3943 for concert line. www.tipitinas.com. Cover $4–$15, depending on the performer.

Dedicated to the late piano master Prof. Longhair, featured in the movie *The Big Easy,* Tip's was long *the* New Orleans club. Though its star has faded considerably, it remains a reliable place for top local bands.

4 The Bar Scene

You won't have any trouble finding a place to drink in New Orleans. Heck, thanks to "to go" (or "geaux") cups, you won't have to spend a minute without a drink in your hand. Certainly, New Orleans provides some of the most convivial, quaint, or downright eccentric places to do so; in many cases, the places are worth going to even if you plan to imbibe nothing stronger than a soda.

THE FRENCH QUARTER & THE FAUBOURG MARIGNY

In addition to the places below, you might consider the clubby bar at **Dickie Brennan's Steakhouse,** 716 Iberville St. (☎ **504/522-2467**), a place where manly men go to drink strong drinks, smoke smelly cigars (they have a vast selection for sale) and chat up girlie girls. Or you could try the low-key sophistication found at **Beque's at the Royal Sonesta,** 300 Bourbon St. (☎ **504/586-0300**), where there is usually a jazz trio playing.

Apple Barrel. 609 Frenchmen St. ☎ **504/949-9399.** No cover.

A small, dusty, wooden-floored watering hole, complete with jukebox and darts where you can find refuge from the hectic Frenchmen scene—or gear up to join in.

The Bombay Club. 830 Conti St. ☎ **504/586-0972.** No cover.

This posh piano bar features jazz Wednesday through Saturday evenings. On Fridays and Saturdays, the music runs past 1am. Apart from the piano, the Bombay Club is a restaurant and a martini bar—in fact, the Bombay's martinis are hailed as the best in town.

Carousel Bar & Lounge. In the Monteleone Hotel, 214 Royal St. ☎ **504/523-3341.** No cover.

There is piano music here Tuesdays through Saturdays, but the real attraction is the bar itself—it really is a carousel, and it really does revolve.

Crescent City Brewhouse. 527 Decatur St. ☎ **504/522-0571.**

When this place opened in 1991, it was the first new brewery in New Orleans in more than 70 years. The equipment is visible to patrons (you can't miss it) and is about as shiny and stylish as light manufacturing can possibly be. Crescent City has a full menu and a weekday happy hour, which brings two-for-one beer specials.

Feelings. 2600 Chartres. ☎ **504/945-2222.** Cover varies.

A low-key, funky neighborhood restaurant and hangout, set around a classic New Orleans courtyard, which is where most drink—unless they are hanging out with the fabulous piano player, singing the night away.

Hard Rock Cafe. 418 N. Peters St. ☎ **504/529-5617.** No cover.

Gag. Better burgers and better beer are to be found elsewhere. Go there instead.

Kerry Irish Pub. 331 Decatur St. ☎ **504/527-5954.** No cover.

This traditional Irish pub has a variety of beers and other spirits, but is most proud of its properly poured pints of Guinness and hard cider. The pub is a good bet for live Irish and "alternative" folk music; it's also a place to throw darts and shoot pool.

♻ **Lafitte's Blacksmith Shop.** 941 Bourbon St. ☎ **504/523-0066.** No cover.

It's some steps away from the main action on Bourbon, but you'll know Lafitte's when you see it. Dating from the 1770s, it's the oldest building in the Quarter—possibly in the Mississippi Valley (though that's not documented)—and looks it. In other towns, this would be a tourist trap. Here, it feels authentic. Definitely worth swinging by, even if you don't drink.

Napoleon House Bar & Cafe. 500 Chartres St. ☎ **504/524-9752.** No cover.

Set in a landmark building, the Napoleon House is just the place to go to have a quiet drink (as opposed to the very loud drinks found elsewhere in the Quarter), and maybe hatch some schemes.

O'Flaherty's Irish Channel Pub. 514 Toulouse St. ☎ **504/529-1317.** No cover.

Over the years, New Orleans' Irish Channel (uptown along Magazine Street) has become visibly less Irish in character. O'Flaherty's is taking up some of the slack. This is the place to go hear the best in local Celtic music, and on Saturdays there's also Irish dancing.

Planet Hollywood. 620 Decatur St. ☎ **504/522-7826.** No cover.

See the description of the Hard Rock Cafe, and add the phrase "only worse."

The R Bar and Royal Street Inn. 1431 Royal St. ☎ **504/948-7499.** No cover.

The R (short for Royal Street) Bar is a little taste of New York's East Village in the Faubourg Marigny. It is a quintessential neighborhood bar in a neighborhood full of artists, wannabe artists, punk rock intellectuals, urban gentrifiers, and well-rounded hipsters. On certain nights, you can get a haircut and a drink for $10. It's just a cool little bar.

OUTSIDE THE FRENCH QUARTER

In addition to those listed below, check out the bar at the International House hotel which is already becoming a lively, hip and happening hangout.

Pat O'Brien's & the Mighty Hurricane

Pat O'Brien's, 718 St. Peter St. (☎ **504/525-4823**), is world famous for the gigantic, rum-based drink with the big-wind name. The formula (according to legend) was stumbled upon by bar owners Charlie Cantrell and George Oechsner while they were experimenting with Caribbean rum during the Second World War. The drink is served in signature 29-ounce hurricane lamp–style glasses. The bar now offers a 3-gallon Magnum Hurricane that stands taller than many small children. It's served with a handful of straws and takes a group to finish (we profoundly hope)—all of whom must drink standing up. Naturally, the offerings and reputation attract the tourists and college yahoos in droves. Some nights the line can stretch out the door and down the street, which seems quite silly given how many other drinking options there are mere feet away.

Which is not to say that Pat's isn't worth a stop—it's a reliable, rowdy, friendly introduction to New Orleans. Just don't expect to be the only person who thinks so. Even if it is a gimmick, what trip to New Orleans is complete without sampling the famous Hurricane? There's no minimum and no cover, but if you buy a drink and it comes in a glass, you'll be paying for the glass until you turn it in at the register for a $2 refund.

Acadian Brewing Company and Beer Garden. 201 N. Carrollton Ave. ☎ **504/483-9003.**

If you want to sample beers from a variety of regional brewing companies, head here. In its first few years, Acadian has won a lot of loyal beer drinkers, and the beer garden has become a favorite Mid City hangout.

The Bulldog. 3236 Magazine St. ☎ **504/891-1516.** No cover.

The Bulldog has become a favored hangout for uptown's young postcollege and young professional crowd (though some frat-party types can still sneak in). It is likely drawn by the bar's beer selection—at more than 50 brews, probably the best in town.

Hyttops Sports Bar & Grill. In the Hyatt Regency, 500 Poydras Plaza. ☎ **504/561-1234.** No cover.

Hyttops is in the lobby of the Hyatt, which is connected to the Superdome, the arena of the Sugar Bowl and New Orleans Saints home games. Everywhere you turn in the bar there's a television (many of them big-screens) featuring some athletic event.

Madigan's. 800 S. Carrollton Ave. ☎ **504/866-9455.** No cover most nights.

In the uptown section of New Orleans, Madigan's is a casual watering hole that has been home to blues musician John Mooney on Sundays.

Nick's. 2400 Tulane Ave. ☎ **504/821-9128.** No cover.

The slogan here is "Looks like the oldest bar in town!"—and it does. Behind the barroom you'll find billiards and occasional performances by live musicians.

The Polo Lounge. In the Windsor Court hotel, 300 Gravier St. ☎ **504/523-6000.** No cover.

The Windsor Court is, without a doubt, the city's finest hotel, and the Polo Lounge is the place to go if you're feeling particularly stylish. Sazeracs and cigars are popular here.

✪ **Saturn Bar.** 3067 St. Claude Ave. ☎ **504/949-7532.** No cover.

Genuine barflies or just slumming celebs? It's so hard to tell when they are passed out in the crumbling booths or blending in with the pack-rat collection that passes as decor. The Saturn Bar is among the hipster set's most beloved dives.

Sazerac Bar and Grill. In the Fairmont Hotel, University Place. ☎ **504/529-4733.** No cover.

In the posh Fairmont Hotel, Sazerac Bar is frequented by the city's young professionals and was featured in the movie *The Pelican Brief.* The African walnut bar and murals by Paul Ninas complete the upscale atmosphere. Wines and champagnes are available by the glass, and a dessert menu is available.

Snake & Jake's Xmas Club Lounge. 7612 Oak St. ☎ **504/861-2802.**

Though admittedly off the beaten path, this tiny, friendly dive is the perfect place for those looking for an authentic neighborhood bar. *Gambit* readers voted Jose the bartender the best in the city.

St. Joe's Bar. 5535 Magazine St. ☎ **504/899-3744.**

An agreeably dark (but not pretentious), nonseedy corner bar, this is a very typical New Orleans friendly-but-not-overbearing place.

Vic's Kangaroo Cafe. 636 Tchoupitoulas St. ☎ **504/524-4329.** No cover.

Despite the perplexing Australian gimmick, this is a friendly bar that caters to the local after-work crowd. On Friday and Saturday nights, decent—and occasionally better than that—blues and R&B acts play with no cover charge.

5 Burlesque & Strip Clubs

As if there weren't enough to Bourbon Street, what with the booze and the music and the booze, there is the sex industry. Kind of. In addition to numerous stores offering what we will euphemistically call marital aids, there are quite a few strip joints—some topless, some bottomless, some offering "live sex acts." If you make a habit of such places, you'll be in heaven. If you are merely curious, or simply in the mood for a naughty evening, this might be the time and place to try one.

Below are a couple of recommendable institutions on this stretch of Bourbon Street (they're two of the tamer ones as well).

Chris Owens Club. 735 St. Louis St. (corner of Bourbon St.). ☎ **504/523-6400.** Cover $11 for shows Wed and Fri 10pm (includes Chris Owens show and 1 drink; $36 for shows Mon, Thurs, and Sat 9:30pm (includes Chris Owens and Al Hirt show and 1 drink). Group rates available.

If you like your entertainment on the sexy side but aren't quite game for Bourbon Street's strippers, this is the place to go. The illustrious Chris Owens, backed by a great group of musicians, puts on a show of fun-filled jazz, popular, country and western, and blues music while revealing enough of her physical endowments to make strong men bay at the moon.

Rick's Cabaret. 315 Bourbon St. ☎ **504/524-4222.** Mon–Sat 11:30pm–4am. Cover $10, women free with male escort. No drink minimum. "Pedestal" dancing $20.

Rick's goes for the classy approach—the grand staircase entrance and rotating chandeliers are a dead giveaway. It is upscale and friendly enough that adventurous couples could go together without the women feeling too uncomfortable.

6 Gay Nightlife

The gay community is quite strong and visible in New Orleans, and the gay bars are some of the most bustling places in town—full of action nearly 24 hours a day. Below you'll find listings of New Orleans' most popular gay nightspots.

For more information, you can check ***Ambush,*** 828-A Bourbon St. (☎ **504/522-8049;** www.ambushmag.com), a great source for the gay community in New Orleans and for visitors. Once you're in New Orleans, you can call the office or pick up a copy at Tower Records, 408 N. Peters St., in the French Quarter, or Lenny's News, 5420 Magazine St., uptown.

BARS

In addition to those listed below, you might also try the **Golden Lantern,** 1239 Royal St. (☎ **504/529-2860**), a nice neighborhood spot where the bartender knows the patrons by name. It's the second oldest gay bar in town. If Levi's and leather are your scene, the **Rawhide,** 740 Burgundy St. (☎ **504/525-8106**), is your best bet; during Mardi Gras, it hosts a great gay costume contest that's not to be missed.

The Bourbon Pub–Parade Disco. 801 Bourbon St. ☎ **504/529-2107.**

This is more or less the most centrally located of the gay bars—it's right at Ground Zero and many of the other popular gay bars are nearby. The downstairs pub offers a video bar; Parade is upstairs and features a high-tech dance floor complete with lasers and smoke. It's consistently voted by several sources as a top dance club in all of America.

Café Lafitte in Exile. 901 Bourbon St. ☎ **504/522-8397.** No cover.

This is one of the oldest gay bars in the United States, having been around since 1953. There's a bar downstairs, and upstairs you'll find a pool table and a balcony that overlooks Bourbon Street. The whole shebang is open 24 hours daily. Come Sunday evening for "Trash Disco."

Good Friends Bar & Queens Head Pub. 740 Dauphine St. ☎ **504/566-7191.** No cover.

This congenial bar and pub often wins the Gay Achievement Award for Best Neighborhood Gay Bar. Downstairs there is a mahogany bar and a pool table. Upstairs is the quiet Queens Head Pub.

LeRoundup. 819 St. Louis St. ☎ **504/561-8340.** No cover.

LeRoundup attracts the most diverse crowd around. You'll find transsexuals lining up at the bar with drag queens and well-groomed men in khakis and Levi's. Expect encounters with working boys. It's open 24 hours.

DANCE CLUBS

In addition to those listed below, you might also try **The Red Room** (see "Jazz & Blues Clubs," above), for some 1940s jazz swing dancing.

Oz. 800 Bourbon St. ☎ **504/593-9491.**

One of New Orleans' newest gay dance clubs, Oz is the place to see and be seen, with a primarily young crowd. It was ranked the city's number-one dance club by *Gambit* magazine, and *Details* magazine named it one of the top 50 clubs in the country. The music is great, there's an incredible laser light show, and from time to time there are go-go boys atop the bar. There are frequent theme nights here, so call ahead if you're going and want to dress accordingly.

✪ **Rubyfruit Jungle.** 640 Frenchmen St. ☎ **504/947-4000.** Cover $3 Fri, $5 Sat; no cover weeknights.

Though it's technically a lesbian bar and dance club, all are welcome here—it's a very friendly, attitude-free establishment.

Wolfendale's. 834 N. Rampart St. ☎ **504/523-7764.**

Popular with the city's gay African American population, Wolfendale's has a courtyard, a raised dance floor, and a pool table. Most don't come to lounge around in the courtyard or by the pool table—people come here to dance. Take a cab.

7 Gambling

The **Harrah's casino** project finally appears to be lurching toward completion. At press time, its opening was planned for October 1999. Feelings are mixed around town about this. The place could either change the tenor of the city completely, for good or for ill, or it could just be met with round indifference. New Orleans does not lack for decadence already; better you should go to Vegas for gambling of that sort. But if you feel you must go, the casino is located at 512 S. Peters St. (☎ **504/533-6016**).

There's also riverboat gambling. Outside the city you can find the **Boomtown Belle Casino** (☎ **504/366-7711** for information and directions), on the West Bank; the **Treasure Chest Casino** (☎ **504/443-8000**), docked on Lake Pontchartrain in Kenner; and **Bally's Casino** (☎ **504/248-3200**), docked on the south shore of Lake Pontchartrain.

9

Cajun Country

*I*ts official name is Acadiana, and it consists of a rough triangle of Louisiana made up of 22 parishes (counties), from St. Landry Parish at the top of the triangle to the Gulf of Mexico at its base. Lafayette is its "capital," and it's dotted with such towns as St. Martinville, New Iberia, Abbeville, and Eunice. You won't find its boundaries on any map, nor the name "Acadiana" stamped across it. But those 22 parishes are Cajun country, and its history and culture are unique in America.

1 Planning Your Trip to Cajun Country

A circular drive will allow you to take in one or two of the plantation homes en route to Baton Rouge (if you take the River Road instead of I-10) before turning west on I-10 to reach Lafayette and the land of the Cajuns. Go north of Lafayette on I-49 to reach Opelousas; Eunice is about 20 minutes west of there on Highway 190. A return to New Orleans on U.S. 90 is a trip through the history, legend, and romance of this region. There is more than a day's worth of interest in this area, so you'll probably want to plan at least an overnight stay. On I-10, the distance from New Orleans to Lafayette 134 miles; Lafayette to New Orleans on U.S. 90 is 167 miles. Listed below are some of the things you should not miss, but you will find scores of other Cajun country attractions on your own. Also listed are some of the outstanding Cajun restaurants (rest assured, bad restaurants do not last long) and places to stay overnight.

Contact the **Lafayette Parish Convention and Visitors Commission Center,** P.O. Box 52066, Lafayette, LA 70505 (☎ **800/346-1958** in the U.S., 800/543-5340 in Canada, or 318/232-3737; fax 318/232-0161). It will send you tons of detailed information to make your trip even more fun. The office is open weekdays 8:30am to 5pm, weekends 9am to 5pm. (See "Lafayette," below.)

Hands down, the best time to visit Acadiana is during festival time (see chapter 2). You'll have a terrific time along with native Cajuns, who enjoy their festivals with real gusto. If you miss this, however, every weekend seems to bring a smaller festival somewhere in the area—and there is always plenty of music to go around at any time of the year.

TOURS

If you can't find time for an extended visit to Cajun country, a 1-day guided tour can provide an introduction to the area. **Tours by Isabelle** (☎ 504/391-3544), specializes in small tours in a comfortable, air-conditioned minivan. You'll cross the Mississippi to visit Cajun country and then take a 2-hour narrated swamp tour. The Cajun Bayou Tour ($50) leaves New Orleans at 1pm and returns around 5:30pm. Isabelle's Grand Tour includes the Cajun Bayou Tour, a guided tour of Oak Alley Plantation, lunch, and a stop in front of Destrehan Plantation.

2 Exploring Cajun Country

BREAUX BRIDGE

Just off I-10 on La. 31, this little town, founded in 1859, prides itself on being the "Crawfish Capital of the World." Its Crawfish Festival and Fair has drawn as many as 100,000 to the town of 4,500, and it's quite the event, with music, a unique parade, crawfish races, crawfish-eating contests, and lots more. It's held the first week in May.

ACCOMMODATIONS

✪ **Maison Des Amis.** 1111 Washington, Breaux Bridge, LA 70517. ☎ **318/ 332-6966.** Fax 318/332-5273. 4 units; 2 without private bathrooms. $75–$95 double. Rates include breakfast. AE, DISC, MC, V.

Voted "Inn of the Month" in the January 1998 issue of *Travel & Leisure,* and the winner of a national preservation award, Maison des Amis offers small but gorgeously appointed rooms. They're in a one-story Creole Caribbean cabin (1860) perched almost on the bayou. The furnishings are a mix of antiques (with at least one delightful wood canopy bed from the 1700s), with modern but appropriate fabric hangings. One room has twin beds and the best view of the bayou. Some of the bathrooms are tiny and require a walk down the glassed-in porch (robes are provided). The two front rooms have private bathrooms (they also have the biggest windows). There is one TV, with a VCR and a collection of old movies.

DINING

Cafe Des Amis. 140 E. Bridge St. ☎ **318/332-5273.** Main courses $7.95– $19.95. AE, DISC, MC, V. Tues–Wed 8am–3pm, Thurs–Fri 8am–10pm, Sat 7:30am–10pm, Sun 7:30am–3pm. Sat mornings feature "Zydeco Breakfast" 8:30–11:30am. CAJUN.

This is an airy, traditional Louisiana space turned modern cafe, with the scribbled thoughts of visitors on the walls, which also feature local folk art. There's also an interesting display of local antiquities. The civic-minded owners (who also own the inn upstairs) are often found treating honors students or local artists at the cafe. Much of what is on the menu is healthy; a grilled shrimp salad was spicy, fresh, and generous with the shrimp, while the étouffée was what that dish should be.

Crawfish Town U.S.A. 2815 Grand Point Hwy. ☎ **318/667-6148.** Reservations recommended. Main courses $4.95–$18.95. AE, DISC, MC, V. Daily 11am–closing. From Lafayette, take I-10 to Henderson (Exit 115). Go north half a mile and follow the signs; you can't miss it. SEAFOOD/CAJUN.

See if you can guess what the house specialty is here. The food is as pleasant as the heavily decorated dining room, and prepared to your taste: mild, strong, or extra-hot. The staff says they serve the biggest crawfish in the world—and who is to challenge them?

EUNICE

Founded in 1894 by C. C. Duson, who named the town for his wife, Eunice is a prairie town. On Saturday nights, **Gilton's Club,** 175 Janet Rd. (at Highway 90 East, about 3 miles east of Eunice; ☎ 318/457-1241), is a genuine Cajun dance hall. A long, cavernous room with misspelled signs and Christmas lights passing for decor, this is where to find the real Cajun dance tradition. Admission is as little as $3, the locals are friendly, food is served, and the dance floor is large. By all means, use it.

ATTRACTIONS & DISTRACTIONS

✪ **Acadian Cultural Center.** 250 West Park. ☎ **318/262-6862.** Free admission; donations accepted. Mon–Sat 8am–5pm.

An almost-perfect example of a small museum, the Acadian Cultural Center is devoted to Cajun life and culture. Exhibits explain everything from the history of the Cajuns to how they worked, played, and got married. The graphics are lively and very readable, well combined with the objects on display (most acquired from local families who have owned them for generations). The center has a collection of videos about Cajun life and will show any and all in the small theater (just ask).

✪ **Liberty Theater.** 2nd and Park. ☎ **318/457-6577.** Admission $3 and up.

This classic 1927 theater has been lovingly restored and turned into a showcase for Cajun music. There's live music most nights, but Saturday attracts the big crowds, for the "Rendezvous des Cajuns" radio show. From 6 to 8pm, Cajun historian and folklorist Barry Ancelet hosts a live program, simulcast on local radio, that features Cajun and zydeco bands. It includes anything from up-and-comers to some of the biggest names, folktales, and jokes. Oh, and it's all in French. Locals and tourists alike pack the seats and aisles, with dancing on the sloped floor by the stage. Don't understand what's being said? As Barry points out, turn to your neighbors—they will be happy to translate.

✪ **Savoy Music Center.** Hwy. 190 East (3 miles east of Eunice). ☎ **318/457-9563.** Tues–Sat 9am–noon, Tues–Fri 1:30–5pm.

On weekdays this is a working music store, with instruments, accessories, and a small but essential selection of Cajun and zydeco CDs and tapes. In the back is the workshop where musician Marc Savoy lovingly crafts his Acadian accordions. On most Saturday mornings, though, this nondescript kelly green building on the outskirts of Eunice is the spiritual center of Cajun music. Keeping alive a tradition that dates from way before electricity, Marc and his wife, Ann, host a jam session where you can hear some of the region's finest music and watch the tunes being passed down from generation to generation. Meanwhile, nonmusical guests munch on hunks of boudin sausage and sip beer while listening or socializing. All comers are welcome, but don't come empty-handed—a pound of boudin or a six-pack of something is appropriate.

ACCOMMODATIONS

If the following are booked, you might also try the **Best Western,** 1531 W. Laurel Ave., in Eunice (☎ **318/457-2800**).

Poiter's Prairie Cajun Inn. 110 W. Park, Eunice, LA 70535. ☎ **318/457-0440.** 9 units. A/C TV TEL. $60 double. AE, DC, DISC, MC, Optima, V.

Its bright pink exterior indicates that this tiny B&B is a bit heavy on the cute, but the location can't be beat—just a half-block from the Liberty Theater and the Acadian Cultural Center. The tiny rooms are technically suites—itty-bitty sitting areas with separate, even smaller bedrooms and full kitchens, all decorated (again, think cutesy) by local Cajun craftsmen. A variety of snacks and breakfast foods (cereal, pastries, fruit, yogurt) are provided nightly. There is also a conference room, and each suite has a computer modem hookup. For a minimal fee, the inn provides transportation to and from the Lafayette airport. Baby-sitting is available.

✪ **Seale Guesthouse.** 125 Seale Lane (off Hwy. 13), Eunice, LA 70535. ☎ **318/457-3753.** 6 units, 4 with private bathroom (1 room's bathroom is across the hall). $75 double. Rates include continental breakfast weekdays, full breakfast weekends. MC, V.

Owner Mark Seale took an abandoned farmhouse and turned it into this wonderful B&B, perfect for a relaxing getaway. Eunice is only a 5-minute drive away, but the guest house and grounds are so inviting, sometimes it's hard to leave. Rooms are decorated with antiques, and with their high ceilings, wood trim, and cozy furniture, each is more attractive and charming than the last. Wide verandas allow you to sit and gaze at the pretty landscaping. This is a hands-off guest house; Mark is happy to give you all kinds of good advice about local doings, but the sheets aren't changed every day, and there's no receptionist. It's perfect if you want privacy.

DINING

D.I.'s Cajun Restaurant. Hwy. 97, Basile. ☎ **318/432-5141.** Main courses $6.75–$12.45. AE, MC, V. Lunch Mon–Fri 10:30am–1:30pm, Tues–Sat 5–11pm. Hwy. 190 to Hwy. 97, then 8 miles south. CAJUN.

Even when you follow the directions to D.I.'s Cajun Restaurant, you will think you are about to drive off the face off the earth. You'll know you're there when you see all the cars in the gravel parking lot. Located on a back highway, D.I.'s is more or less what Mulate's was before the tourists found it: a homey family restaurant full of locals dancing to live music (except Thursday) and stuffing themselves with crawfish and catfish.

Matilda's. Hwy. 190 and St. Mary. ☎ **318/546-0329.** $3.50–$10.80. MC, V. Tues–Thurs 11am–7pm, Fri 11am–10pm, Sat 11:30am–8pm, Sun 11am–3pm. BARBECUE.

For barbecue with all the fixings, this is the one sit-down place in town. It's a wood shack that some might call "quaint" but others know is authentic. The many side dishes vary in quality, but the barbecue, while not all that spicy, is agreeable.

Ruby's Cafe. 221 W. Walnut Ave. ☎ **318/457-2583.** All items under $5. Mon–Sat 5am–5pm. No credit cards. CAJUN/SOUL FOOD.

Located in the center of Eunice, Ruby's is where the real people hang out. Nothing fancy, and we mean nothing—but in the best of all ways. Got a hankering for roast chicken or, better still, ponce (stuffed cow stomach—it's better than it sounds)? Come here.

Shopping

Music Machine. 235 W. Walnut Ave. ☎ **318/457-4846.** Daily 9am to at least 7pm.

Owner Todd Ortego claims this is the "only record store, snow cone, and pool place in the area" and he gets no dispute from us. The store features a pretty good selection of local music (on CD and cassette), and the employees should be able to help you figure out what to buy if you need guidance. Outside of Floyd's in Ville Platte, this is probably your best music resource. Todd is also a local DJ (you can find him on the radio playing zydeco and South Louisiana party music), and he's in the store during the week. If you are coming for a weekend of music, drop by and ask him where to go—by Thursday, he usually knows what's going on.

Boudin Joints

Boudin is Cajun sausage, made of pork usually mixed with rice and stuffed inside a chewy casing. If it's done right, it's spicy and sublime. Try for yourself—it's a cheap (just over $2 a pound), filling snack. It's easy to find, but we recommend the following place.

✪ **Superette Slaughterhouse,** Bobcat Drive and Maple Avenue, in Eunice (☎ **318/546-6041**), is open Monday to Friday from 6am to 5pm, Saturday from 6am to noon. The name is a little unnerving to those of us from urban areas, but the locals swear this is the best boudin around, and they are probably right.

LAFAYETTE

If you haven't written in advance, make your first stop the **Lafayette Parish Convention and Visitors Commission Center,** 1400 NW Evangeline Thruway (☎ **800/346-1958** in the U.S., 800/543-5340 in Canada, or 318/232-3808). Turn off I-10 at Exit 103A, go south for about a mile, and you'll find the office in the center of the median. It's open weekdays 8:30am to 5pm, weekends 9am to 5pm.

We also highly recommend the **Festival International de Louisiane,** a 6-day music and art festival that many find a good alternative to the increasingly crowded Jazz Fest. While the scope of the bands, naturally, is nothing like the big deal in New Orleans, there's an interesting lineup each year, with an emphasis on music from other French-speaking lands. The Festival takes place in the center of town. In contrast to Jazz Fest, it's low-key and a manageable size. Best of all, it's free! Festival International is held at the end of April; for dates, call or write the Festival International de Louisiane, 735 Jefferson St., Lafayette, LA 70501 (☎ **318/232-8086;** www.fil.net-connect.net).

Music can be found year-round at the **Grant Street Dance Hall,** 113 W. Grant St. (☎ **318/237-8513**). The warehouse-type building features the best in local music, from Cajun to brass bands, and is where out-of-towners are most likely to play. The zydeco hot spot is **El Sido's,** 1523 N. Antoine St. (☎ **318/237-1959**), where combos like Nathan & the Zydeco Cha-Cha's hold sway. Both joints jump, and any night at either is likely to be a good one.

SEEING THE SIGHTS

You shouldn't leave the area without exploring its bayous and swamps. Gliding through misty bayous dotted with gnarled cypress trees that drip Spanish moss, seeing native water creatures and birds in their natural habitat, and learning how Cajuns harvest their beloved crawfish is an experience not to be missed. To arrange a voyage, contact Terry Angelle at **Angelle's Atchafalaya Basin Swamp Tours,** Whiskey River Landing, P.O. Box 111, Cecilla, LA 70521 (☎ **318/228-8567**). His tour gives you nearly 2 hours in the third-largest swamp in the United States, with Cajun guides who have spent their lives thereabouts. There's a glass-enclosed boat for large groups and a small, open boat for up to 14. The fares are $12 for adults, $10 for seniors, $6 for children under 12. Departure times are 10am, 1pm, and 3pm (and 5pm during daylight saving time). To reach Whiskey River Landing from I-10, take Exit 115 to Henderson, go through Henderson to the levee, and turn right. The landing is the fourth exit on the left.

Acadian Village. 200 Greenleaf Dr. ☎ **800/962-9133** or 318/981-2364. Admission $6 adults, $5 seniors, $2.50 children 6–14, free for children under 6. Daily 10am–5pm. Closed major holidays. Take I-10 to Exit 97. Go south on La. 93 to Ridge Rd., turn right, then turn left on West Broussard.

Just south of La. 342, you'll find a reconstructed (actually, reassembled) Cajun bayou community. Houses have been moved from their original locations to this site beside a sleepy bayou, and a footpath on its banks takes you past the historic structures. The buildings hold a representative collection of Cajun furnishings.

Vermilionville. 1600 Surrey St. ☎ **800/99-BAYOU** or 318/233-4077. Fax 318/233-1694. Admission $8 adults, $6.50 seniors, $5 students, free for children under 6. Daily 10am–5pm. Closed Jan 1, Dec 25. Take I-10 to Exit 103A. Take Evangeline Thruway south to Surrey St., then follow signs.

A recent addition to the Lafayette scene is this reconstruction of a Cajun-Creole settlement from the 1765–1890 era. Vermilionville sits on the banks of the brooding Bayou Vermilion, adjacent to the airport on U.S. 90. Hundreds of skilled artisans labored to restore original Cajun homes and to reconstruct others that were typical of such a village. Homes of every level in society are represented, from the humblest to the most well-to-do. The costumed staff in each gives a vivid demonstration of daily life back then, and craftspeople ply their traditional crafts. In the performance center, there is music, plays, dancing, and storytelling.

Alexandre Mouton House/Lafayette Museum. 1122 Lafayette St. ☎ **318/234-2208.** Admission $3 adults, $2 seniors, $1 students. Tues–Sat 9am–5pm, Sun 3–5pm. Closed holidays.

Louisiana's first Democratic governor, Alexandre Mouton, once lived in this antebellum town house with square columns and two galleries. Today it houses the Lafayette Museum. The main house was built in the early 1800s, and the cupola, attic, and second floor were added in 1849. Inside, in addition to the antiques, paintings, and historic documents, there's a colorful collection of Mardi Gras costumes that were worn by Lafayette's krewe kings and queens.

Chretien Point Plantation. 665 Chretien Point Rd., Sunset. ☎ **800/880-7050** or 318/233-7050. Admission $6.50 adults, $6 seniors, $3 children 4–12, free for children under 4. Daily 10am–5pm. Last tour 4pm. Closed holidays. Take I-10 west to Exit 97, then go north about 8 miles. A little over 2 miles north of Cankton, turn left onto Parish Rd. 356 (toward Bristol), then right on Chretien Point Rd.; plantation is about a mile farther, on the left.

One of Cajun country's most intriguing plantation mansions is a short drive (about 15 miles) north of Lafayette. Allow yourself at least an hour to explore the columned home, built in 1831 on a 1776 Spanish land grant. The house is fascinating, and even more so are the tales of past owners. Its history includes links to privateer Jean Lafitte, a flamboyant gambler, his equally flamboyant widow, a ghost or two, a buried treasure (never recovered), and a Civil War battle fought right out front. And if you remember the scene in *Gone With the Wind* when Scarlett O'Hara shoots a marauding Union soldier on the stairs at Tara, you'll recognize the staircase—it was copied for the movie.

The plantation also operates a **bed-and-breakfast.** The rooms are in the manor house; you get a full breakfast and a tour of the mansion, plus use of the pool and tennis courts. Rooms are $95 to $200 per night.

ACCOMMODATIONS

Bois des Chenes Inn. 338 N. Sterling (at Mudd Ave.), Lafayette, LA 70501. ☎ **318/233-7816.** Fax 318/233-7816. www.members.aol.com/boisdchene/bois.htm. 5 units. A/C TV. $95–$135 double. Rates include breakfast. Extra person $30. AE, MC, V.

Now listed on the National Register of Historical Houses, Bois des Chenes was once the center of a 3,000-acre cattle and sugar plantation. Its restoration has been a labor of love. All guest rooms are tastefully furnished with antiques of different periods, and each has a small refrigerator and down pillows. The rates include a Louisiana-style breakfast, a bottle of wine, and a tour of the house. The owner, a retired geologist, conducts nature and birding trips into the Atchafalaya Swamp as well as guided fishing and hunting trips. Book as far in advance as possible.

Holiday Inn Central–Holidome. 2032 NE Evangeline Thruway, Lafayette, LA 70509. ☎ **800/942-4868** or 318/233-6815. 243 units. A/C TV TEL. $69–$79 double. AE, CB, DC, DISC, JCB, MC, V.

This Holiday Inn has superior guest rooms, some of which are equipped for travelers with disabilities. There is a lounge, a coffee shop, a good restaurant, an indoor pool, a whirlpool, a sauna, a game room, lighted tennis courts, a jogging track, a playground, a picnic area, and a gift shop.

Hotel Acadiana. 1801 W. Pinhook Rd., Lafayette, LA 70508. ☎ **800/ 874-4664** in Louisiana, 800/826-8386 in the U.S. and Canada, or 318/233-8120. 296 units. A/C TV TEL. $79–$210 double. AE, DC, DISC, MC, V. From New Orleans, take I-10 west to Exit 103A. Follow Evangeline Thruway to Pinhook Rd., turn right, and follow Pinhook across bridge; hotel is on left.

The Hotel Acadiana is a great value. The rates are low, but you have all the modern conveniences you'd expect to find in a large chain hotel: two double beds or a king in each room, a minirefrigerator, cable TV, and a warm, friendly staff. You'll also be in a central location for sightseeing. Room service, laundry service, concierge service, and a complimentary airport shuttle are provided. Facilities include an outdoor pool and a health club.

Lafayette Hilton & Towers. 1521 Pinhook Rd., Lafayette, LA 70508. ☎ **800/33-CAJUN** or 318/235-6111. www.hilton.com. 327 units. A/C TV TEL. $105–$115 single or double; $185–$300 suite. Weekend, senior, student, faculty, military discounts available. AE, CB, DC, MC, V, DISC.

The centrally located Lafayette Hilton and Towers has nicely appointed guest rooms and suites. Some have private patios. There is a good restaurant overlooking the bayou, a lounge with live music and dancing Monday through Saturday, and a heated pool.

DINING IN & AROUND LAFAYETTE

Café Vermilionville. 1304 Pinhook W. Rd. ☎ **318/237-0100.** Reservations recommended. Main courses $15–$24. AE, DC, DISC, MC, V. Mon–Fri 11am–2pm; Mon–Sat 5:30–10pm. Closed holidays. INTERNATIONAL/CAJUN.

In a beautifully restored historic Acadian building of cypress and handmade brick that dates from 1799, Café Vermilionville has a glassed-in dining room overlooking the courtyard and herb garden. The superb menu represents the best of Louisiana French and Cajun cuisine, with lots of fresh seafood, including specialties like salmon au poivre and Louisiana crawfish.

✪ **Prejean's.** 3480 I 49 North. ☎ **318/896-3247.** Reservations strongly recommended. Children's menu $3.50–$8.95; main courses $12–$24. AE, CB, DC, DISC, MC, V. Sun–Thurs 11am–10pm, Fri–Sat 11am–11pm. Take I-10 to Exit 103B, then I-49 north to U.S. 167 North. Follow the signs—it's next to the Evangeline Downs Racetrack. CAJUN.

Prejean's is still an unpretentious family restaurant with live Cajun music every night. But chef James Graham has turned Prejean's from a fried seafood emporium to one of Acadiana's finest restaurants, showcasing the best ingredients and styles Cajun cuisine has to offer. Seafood is the specialty, with large menu sections devoted to fish, shrimp and oysters, crawfish, and crab dishes, each offered at least a half-dozen ways, and a few alligator dishes. In the unlikely event you have room for dessert, the chocolate Grand Marnier torte is highly recommended.

Prudhomme's Cajun Cafe. 4674 NE Evangeline Thruway, near Carencro. ☎ **318/896-7964.** Reservations recommended. Main courses $6.95–$16.95. AE, DISC, MC, V. Tues–Sat 11am–10pm. Take I-10 to Exit 103B and go north on I-49 to Exit 7 (3 miles past racetrack). Restaurant is on right side of Frontage Rd. CAJUN.

Set in an Acadian country home, this restaurant is run by Enola Prudhomme, who is easily the equal of her famous brother, Paul, in the kitchen. Assisted by her son and two sons-in-law, she serves dishes from a menu that changes daily. Blackened tuna and eggplant pirogue (hollowed out and filled with seafood in a luscious cream sauce) are just two of the specialties. There's ramp access for those who need it.

Randol's Restaurant and Cajun Dance Hall. 2320 Kaliste Saloom Rd. ☎ **800/962-2586** or 318/981-7080. Reservations for 20 or more only. Main courses $7.95–$15.95. MC, V. Mon–Fri 11am–2pm and 5–10pm, Sat–Sun 5–11pm. Closed major holidays. From New Orleans, take I-10 west to Exit 103A. Follow Evangeline Thruway to Pinhook Rd., turn right, and follow Pinhook to Kaliste Saloom Rd. (on the right). Randol's will be on your right. CAJUN.

In addition to better-than-average Cajun food, Randol's offers a good-sized, popular dance floor where dancers are likely to be locals enjoying their own fais-dodo. The star of the menu is seafood, all fresh from bayou or Gulf waters, and served fried, steamed, blackened, or grilled. A house specialty is the seafood platter, which includes a cup of seafood gumbo, fried shrimp, fried oysters, fried catfish, stuffed crab, crawfish étouffée, warm French bread, and coleslaw.

VILLE PLATTE

If you've fallen in love with Cajun music and want to take some home with you, you have a good reason to detour to the town of Ville Platte.

✪ **Floyd's Record Shop.** 434 E. Main St. ☎ **318/367-5622.** Mon–Sat 8:30am–5:30pm.

Floyd Soileau is in some ways the unofficial mayor of Acadiana, and certainly one of its biggest boosters—a sort of one-man chamber of commerce. But he's meant much more to the region as one of the key entrepreneurs of bayou music. Long before Cajun and zydeco were known outside the region, he was recording and releasing the music on three labels: Swallow for Cajun, Maison de Soul for zydeco, and Jin (named after his charming wife) for swamp pop, the regional offshoot of '50s and early '60s pop and soul styles. For fans of the music, this is a must-stop locale, with a fine selection of Floyd's releases by such great artists as D. L. Menard ("The Cajun Hank Williams") and Clifton Chenier (the King of Zydeco), as well as other releases that may be hard to find anywhere else.

DINING

The Pig Stand. 318 E. Main St. ☎ **318/363-2883.** $10.25 and under. No credit cards. Daily 5am–10pm. PIG.

As you might guess, the Pig Stand serves pig. A local institution, it even popped up in the recent Elvis Cole mystery *Voodoo River*, which erroneously described the place as having an outside window and serving boudin. It's a little dump of a local hangout that serves divine barbecued chicken and other Southern specialties for cheap prices. It's a treat—don't miss it. And it's just down the street from Floyd's, in case you worked up an appetite buying music.

Index

See also separate Accommodations, Restaurant indexes, below.

ACCOMMODATIONS